A-Z SOUTHEND

CW01025179

Key to Map Pages	2-3
Map Pages	4-41

Index to
Villages
selected

REFERENCE

A Road	A129
B Road	B1007
Dual Carriageway	
One-way Street Traffic flow on A Roads is also indicated by a heavy line on the driver's left.	
Road Under Construction Opening dates are correct at the time of publication.	
Proposed Road	
Restricted Access	
Pedestrianized Road	
Track / Footpath	
Residential Walkway	
Railway	Station Tunnel Level Crossing
Built-up Area	PARK AV.
Local Authority Boundary	— · — · —
Post Town Boundary	
Postcode Boundary (within Post Town)	— · — · —
Map Continuation	14
Airport	✈

Car Park (selected)	P
Church or Chapel	†
Cycleway (selected)	🚲
Fire Station	■
Hospital	H
House Numbers (A & B Roads only)	57 44
Information Centre	i
National Grid Reference	⁵70
Police Station	▲
Post Office	★
Safety Camera with Speed Limit Fixed cameras and long term road works cameras. Symbols do not indicate camera direction.	30
Toilet: without facilities for the Disabled with facilities for the Disabled	▽ ▽
Educational Establishment	▢
Hospital or Healthcare Building	▢
Industrial Building	▢
Leisure or Recreational Facility	▢
Place of Interest	▢
Public Building	▢
Shopping Centre or Market	▢
Other Selected Buildings	▢

SCALE
1:19,000
3.33 inches (8.47cm) to 1 mile
5.26 cm to 1 kilometre

0	¼	½	¾ Mile
0	250	500	750	1 Kilometre

A-Z AZ AtoZ
registered trade marks of
Geographers' A-Z Map Company Ltd

www. az.co.uk

EDITION 8 2016
Copyright © Geographers' A-Z Map Co. Ltd.
Telephone: 01732 781000 (Enquiries & Trade Sales)
01732 783422 (Retail Sales)

© Crown copyright and database rights 2016 OS 100017302.

Safety camera information supplied by www.PocketGPSWorld.com.
Speed Camera Location Database Copyright 2016 © PocketGPSWorld.com

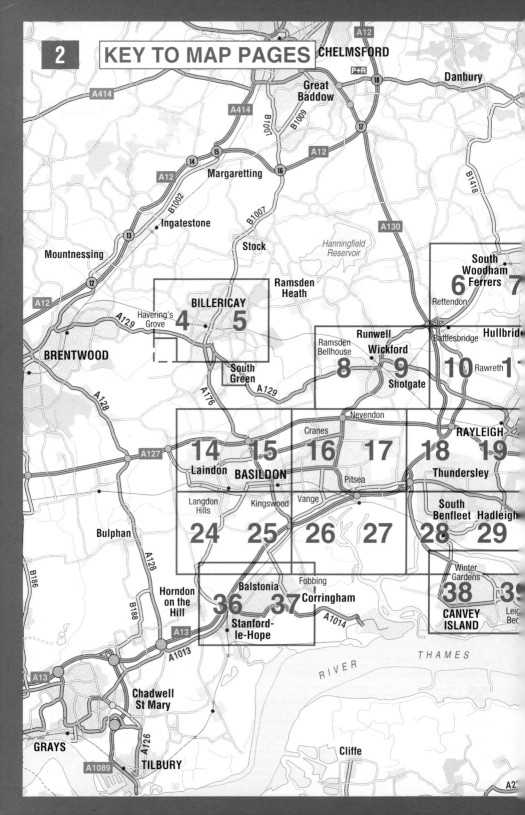

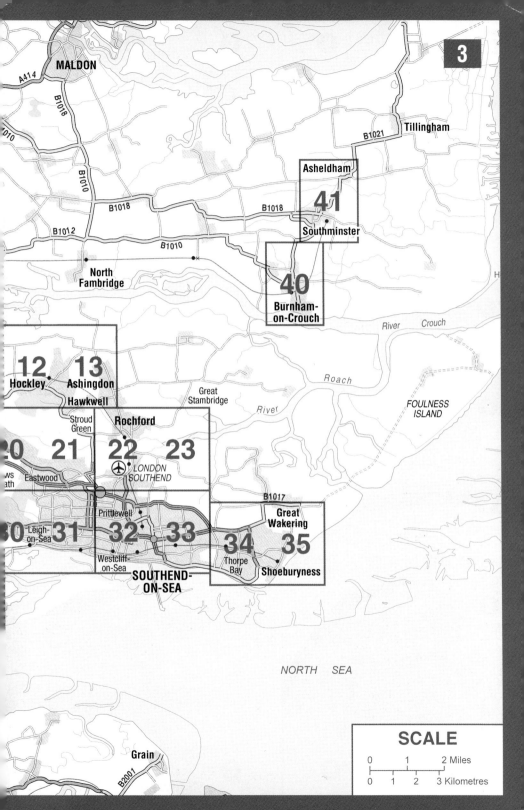

3

A414
MALDON
B1018
1010
B1010
B1018
B1012
B1010

B1021
Tillingham

Asheldham
41
B1018
Southminster

North
Fambridge

40
Burnham-
on-Crouch

River   Crouch

H

Roach
River

FOULNESS
ISLAND

12.
Hockley.
13
Ashingdon
Hawkwell

Great
Stambridge

Stroud
Green
22
Rochford
23

20
ws
ath
21
Eastwood

LONDON
SOUTHEND

B1017

Great
Wakering

30
Leigh-
on-Sea
31
Prittlewell
32
33
34
Thorpe
Bay
35
Shoeburyness

Westcliff-
on-Sea
SOUTHEND-
ON-SEA

NORTH   SEA

Grain
B2001

| SCALE |
| 0   1   2 Miles |
| 0 1 2 3 Kilometres |

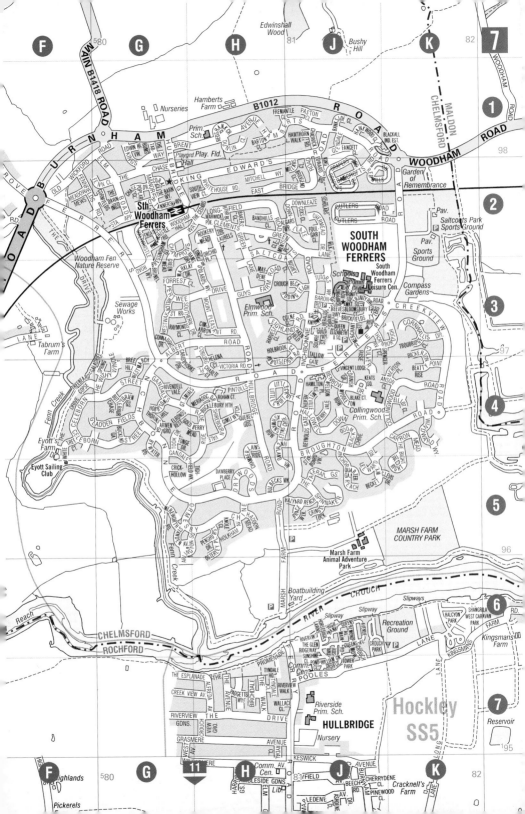

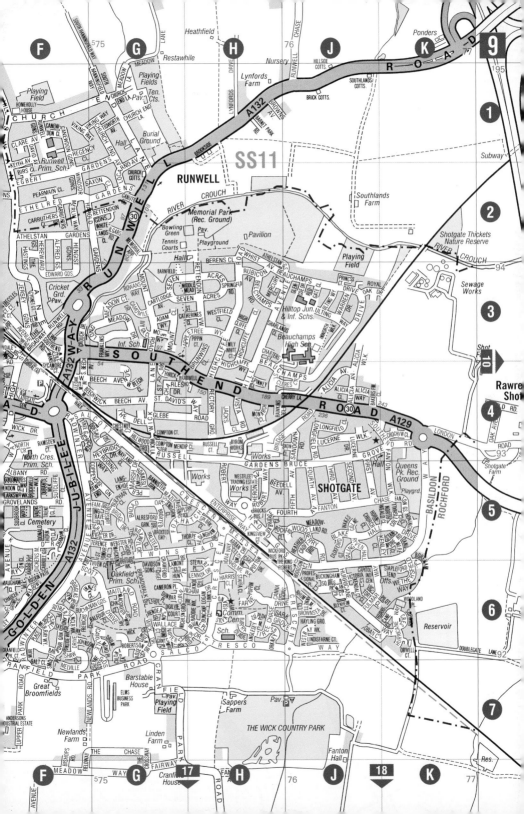

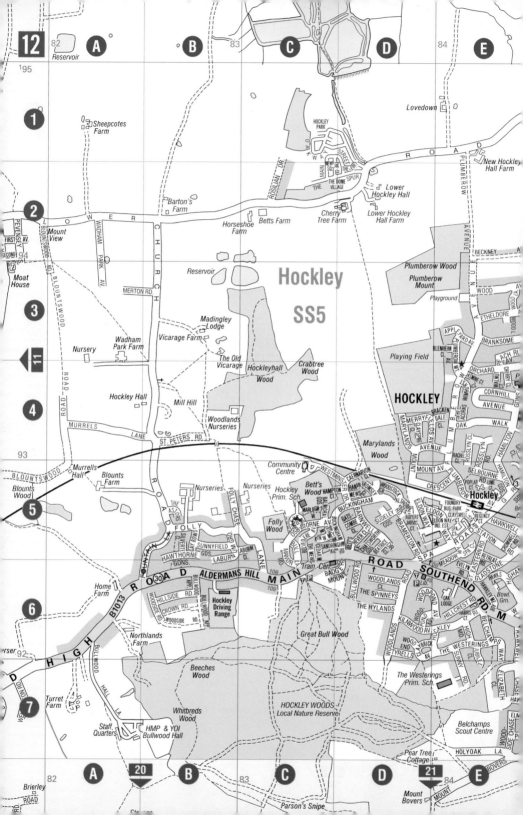

Hockley
SS5

HOCKLEY

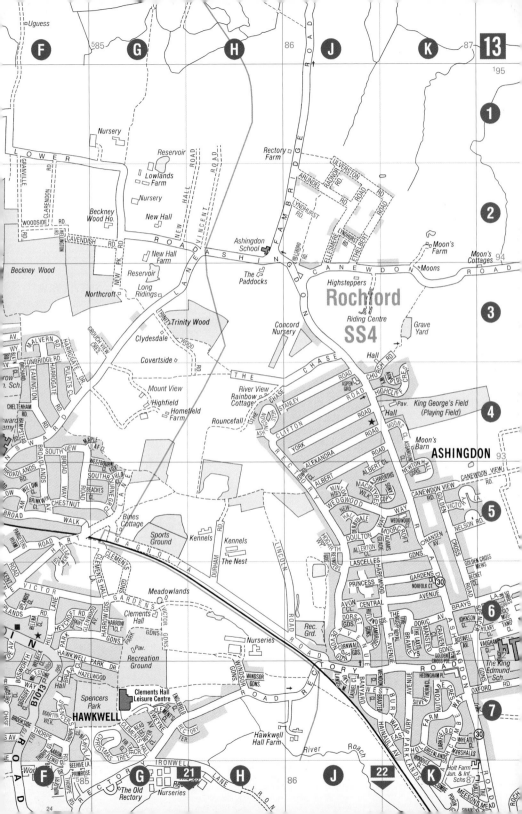

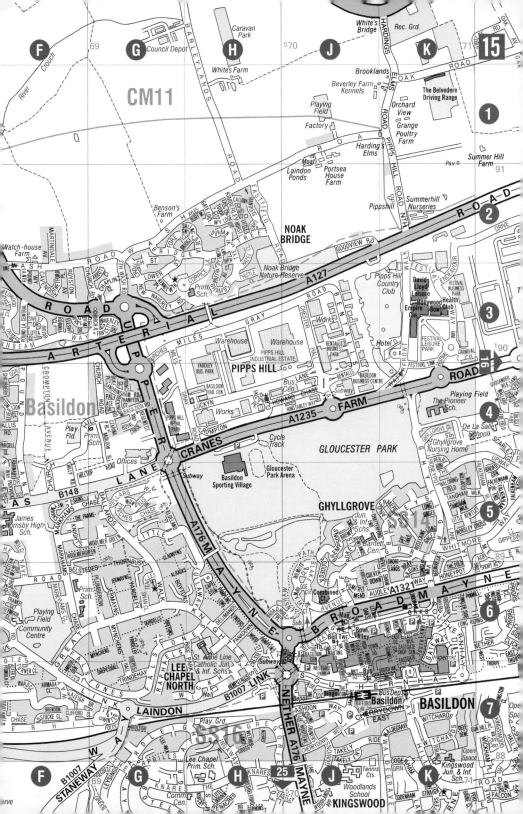

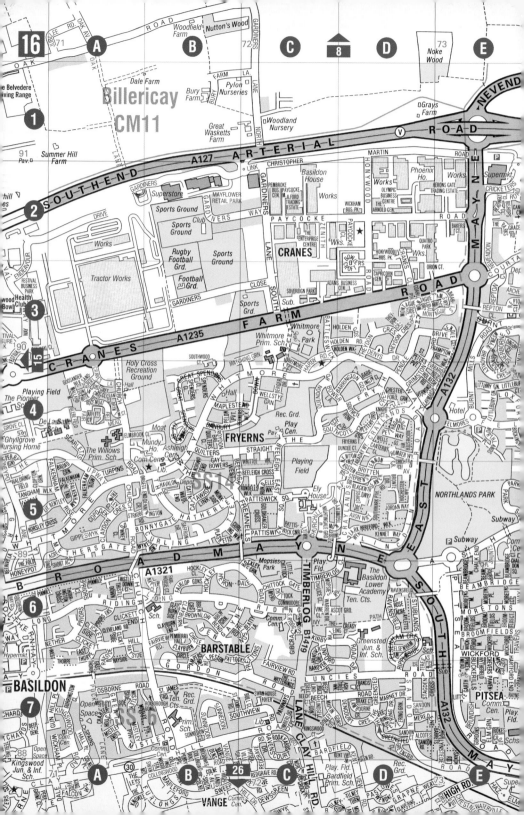

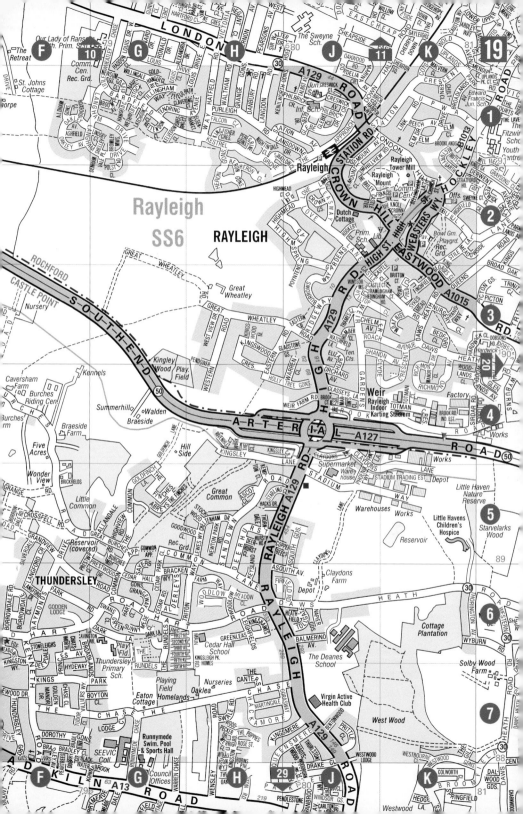

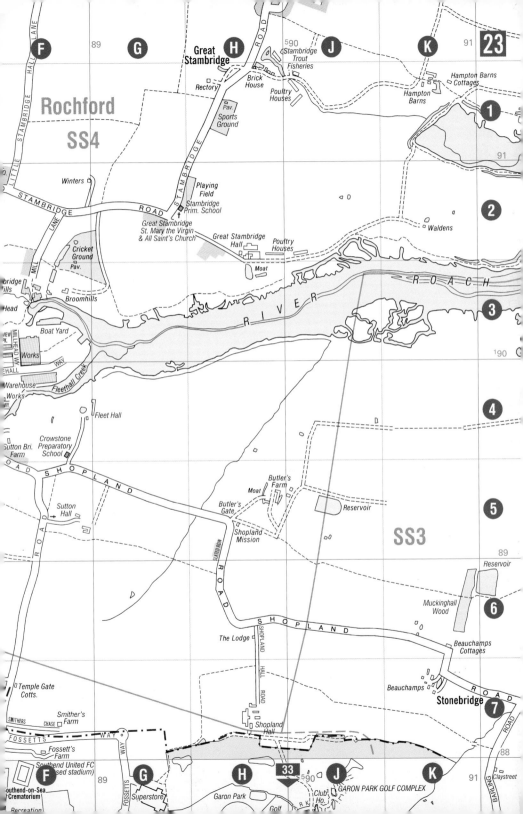

F 89 G **Great Stambridge** H 590 J K 91 91

Rochford

SS4

Hampton Barns Cottages

Stambridge Trout Fisheries

Rectory

Hampton Barns

Brick House

Poultry Houses

Pav. Sports Ground

1

91

Winters

Playing Field

Waldens

Stambridge Prim. School

2

Great Stambridge St. Mary the Virgin & All Saint's Church

Great Stambridge Hall

Poultry Houses

Cricket Ground Pav.

Moat

R O A C H

oridge ills

Broomhills

R I V E R

3

Head

190

EW K

Boat Yard

MILLHEAD W

Works

4

HALL

Warehouse

Works

Fleethall Creek

WAY

Fleet Hall

Sutton Bri. Farm

Crowstone Preparatory School

Butler's Farm

OAD

SHOPLAND

Moat

Reservoir

5

SS3

Sutton Hall

Butler's Gate

Shopland Mission

89

Reservoir

SLATED WAY

6

Muckinghall Wood

SHOPLAND

Beauchamps Cottages

The Lodge

ROAD

SHOPLAND

HALL

Beauchamps

ROAD

Stonebridge 7

Temple Gate Cotts.

Smithers

Smither's Farm

CHASE

FOSSETTS

WAY

Shopland Hall

88

Claystreet

BARLING ROAD

Fossett's Farm

F Southend United FC (sed stadium) 89

Southend-on-Sea Crematorium

FOSSETTS WAY

G Superstore

H 33 590 J

Garon Park

GARON PARK GOLF COMPLEX

K 91

Club Ho.

Recreation

Golf

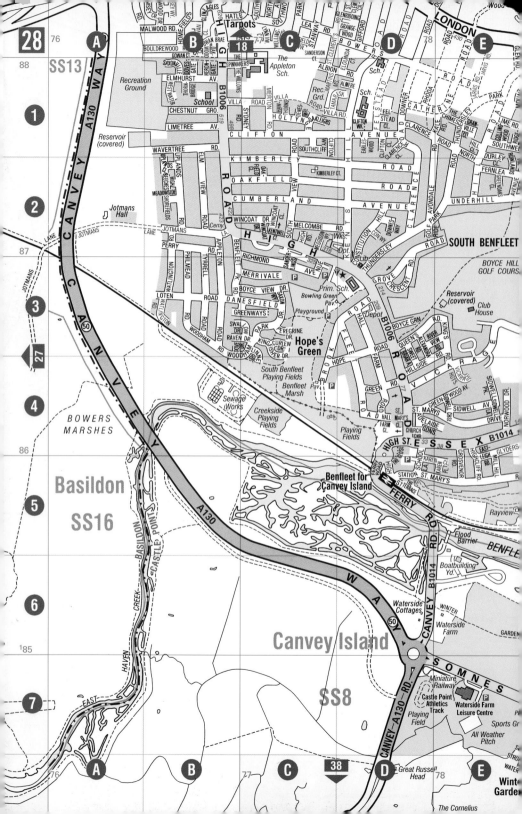

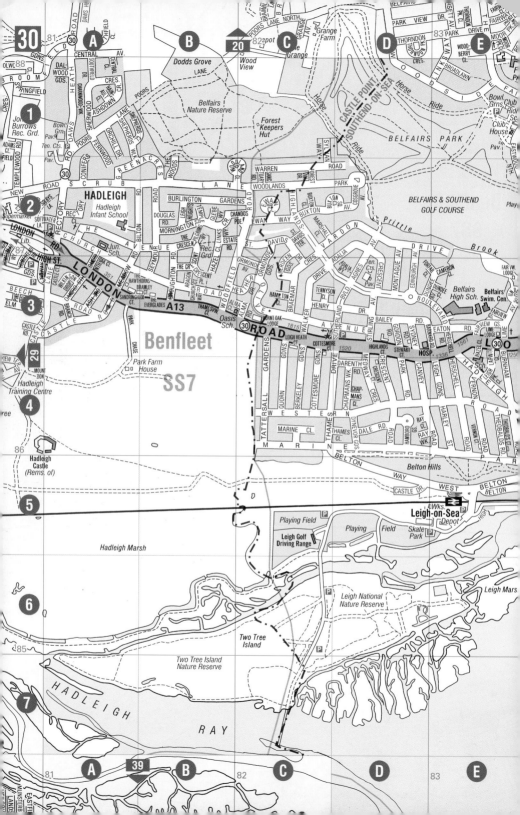

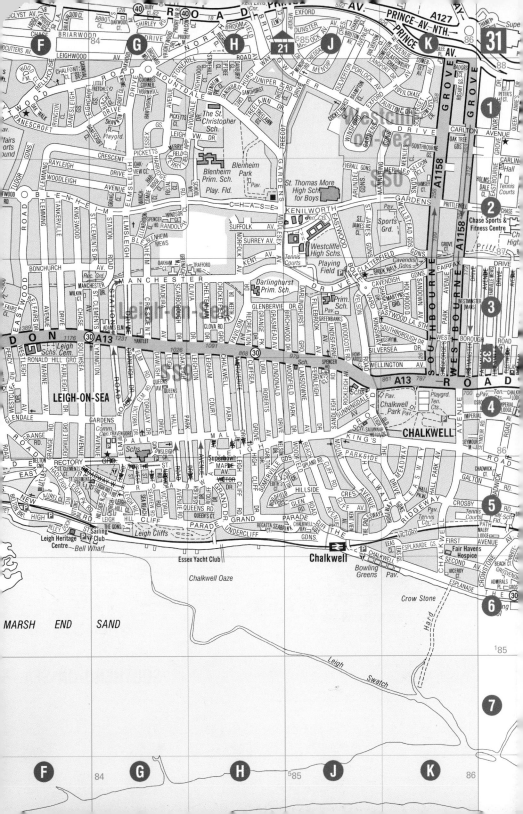

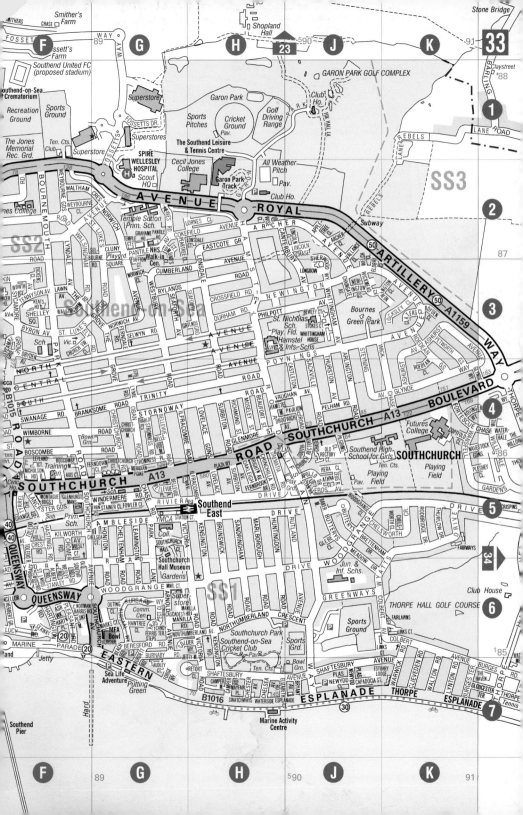

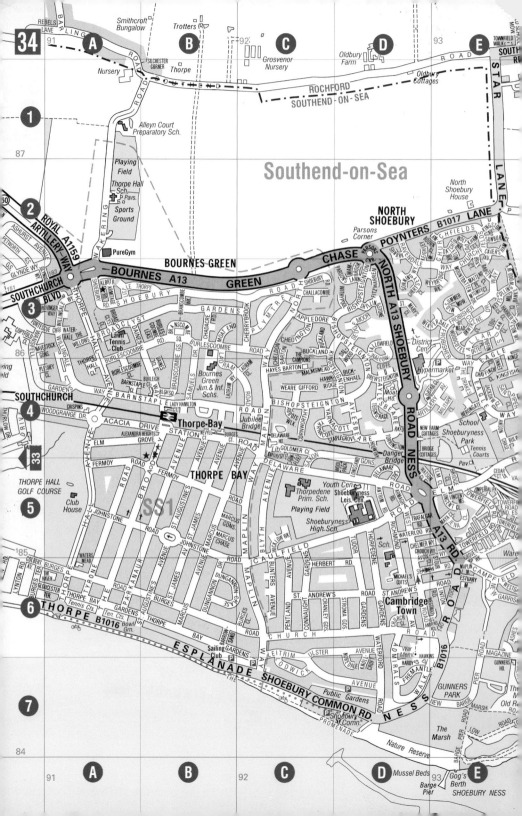

F HIGH B1017

Playing Field
Coronation

324
335

Health Cen.
THE MALLARDS

324

G Exhibition La.

Great Wakering Prim. Sch.

Old Hall La.

Con. Way

GREAT WAKERING

Crouchmans Farm

Crouchmans Cottage

The Lansdowne

Shoebury Nurseries

Great Wakering Common

J Miller's Farm

K Landwick Cottages 96

STAIRS RD.

Samuel's Corner

Morrin's

1

Shoeburyness New Ranges

CHASE

87

DANGER AREA

2

Cupid's Corner

Football Pitches

CHASE

Poynter's Point

3 Black Grounds

86

FRIARS PARK

Friars Prim. Sch.

SS3

New Ranges

Suttons

Old Manor House

Jetties

Pigs Bay

4

Warehouses
Southend Seedbed Cen.

The Vanguards

Causeway

East Beach Caravan Park

5

¹85

Thorpe Green

Shoeburyness

Paddling Pool

N O R T H

S E A

6

SHOEBURYNESS

Landing Slip

DANGER AREA

New Drill Shed

7

84

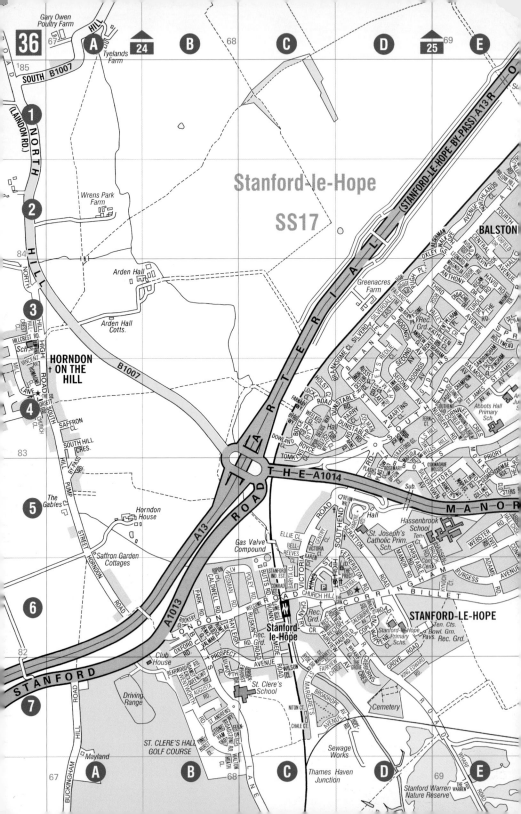

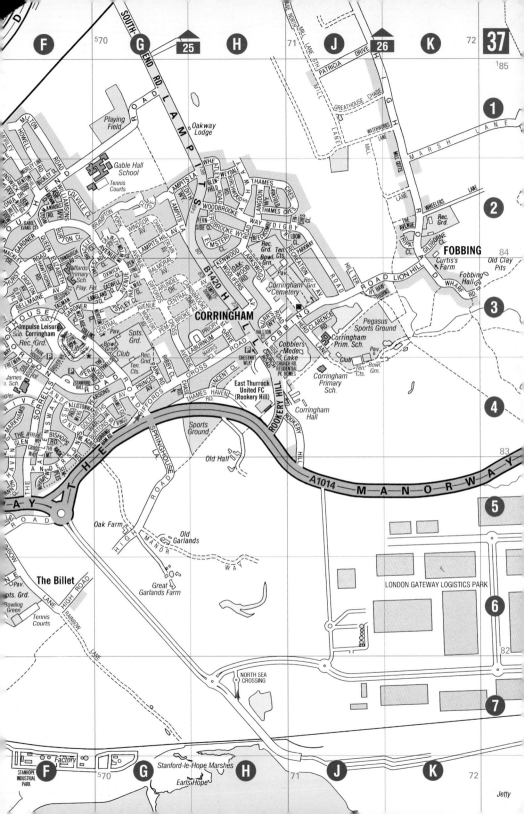

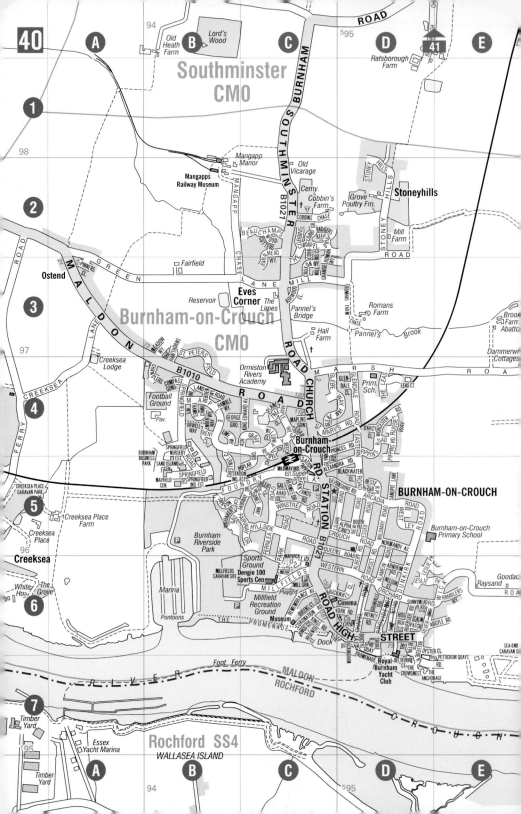

INDEX

Including Streets, Places & Areas, Hospitals etc., Industrial Estates,
Selected Flats & Walkways, Stations and Selected Places of Interest.

HOW TO USE THIS INDEX

1. Each street name is followed by its Postcode District, then by its Locality abbreviation(s) and then by its map reference;
e.g. **Abbotts Dr.** SS17: Stan H . . . .5D **36** is in the SS17 Postcode District and the Stanford-le-Hope Locality and is to be found in square 5D on page **36**. The page number is shown in bold type.

2. A strict alphabetical order is followed in which Av., Rd., St., etc. (though abbreviated) are read in full and as part of the street name; e.g. **Beechcombe** appears after **Beech Cl.** but before **Beech Ct.**

3. Streets and a selection of flats and walkways that cannot be shown on the mapping, appear in the index with the thoroughfare to which they are connected shown in brackets; e.g. **Aimes Grn.** *SS13: Bas* . . . .4G **17** (off Porters)

4. Addresses that are in more than one part are referred to as not continuous.

5. Places and areas are shown in the index in BLUE TYPE and the map reference is to the actual map square in which the town centre or area is located and not to the place name shown on the map; e.g. **ASHINGDON** 6K **13**

6. An example of a selected place of interest is **Burnham-on-Crouch and District Mus.** 6C **40**

7. Examples of stations are:
Battlesbridge Station (Rail) . . . .1B **10**; **Basildon Bus Station** 7J **15**

8. An example of a Hospital, Hospice or selected Healthcare facility is **BASILDON UNIVERSITY HOSPITAL** 2H **25**

GENERAL ABBREVIATIONS

All. : Alley	**Cres.** : Crescent	**Ind.** : Industrial	**Res.** : Residential
App. : Approach	**Cft.** : Croft	**Info.** : Information	**Ri.** : Rise
Arc. : Arcade	**Dr.** : Drive	**La.** : Lane	**Rd.** : Road
Av. : Avenue	**E.** : East	**Lit.** : Little	**Shop.** : Shopping
Blvd. : Boulevard	**Est.** : Estate	**Lwr.** : Lower	**Sth.** : South
Bri. : Bridge	**Fld.** : Field	**Mnr.** : Manor	**Sq.** : Square
Bldgs. : Buildings	**Flds.** : Fields	**Mans.** : Mansions	**St.** : Street
Bus. : Business	**Gdn.** : Garden	**Mkt.** : Market	**Ter.** : Terrace
Cvn. : Caravan	**Gdns.** : Gardens	**Mdw.** : Meadow	**Twr.** : Tower
Cen. : Centre	**Gth.** : Garth	**Mdws.** : Meadows	**Trad.** : Trading
Chu. : Church	**Ga.** : Gate	**M.** : Mews	**Va.** : Vale
Circ. : Circle	**Gt.** : Great	**Mt.** : Mount	**Vw.** : View
Cl. : Close	**Grn.** : Green	**Mus.** : Museum	**Vs.** : Villas
Comn. : Common	**Gro.** : Grove	**Nth.** : North	**Vis.** : Visitors
Cnr. : Corner	**Hgts.** : Heights	**Pde.** : Parade	**Wlk.** : Walk
Cotts. : Cottages	**Ho.** : House	**Pk.** : Park	**W.** : West
Ct. : Court	**Ho's.** : Houses	**Pl.** : Place	**Yd.** : Yard

LOCALITY ABBREVIATIONS

Asheldham: CM0 . . . . .Ashel	**Crays Hill:** CM11 . . . . .C Hill	**Langdon Hills:** SS15-17 . . . . . . .Lan H	**Shoeburyness:** SS3 . . . . .Shoe
Ashingdon: SS4 . . . . .Ashin	**Downham:** CM11 . . . . .D'ham	**Leigh-on-Sea:** SS6-7,SS9 . . . . .Lgh S	**Southend-on-Sea:**
Barling Magna: SS3 . . . . .Barl M	**Dunton:** CM13 . . . . .Dun	**Little Burstead:** CM12 . . . . . . .L Bur	SS1-2,SS4,SS9 . . . . . .Sth S
Basildon: CM12,SS13-16 . . . . . . .Bas	**East Hanningfield:** CM3 . . . . . .E Han	**Little Wakering:** SS3 . . . . . . .L Wak	**Southminster:** CM0 . . . . .S'min
Battlesbridge: SS11 . . . . .Bat	**Fobbing:** SS16-17 . . . . .Fob	**Mountnessing:** CM12 . . . . . . .Mount	**South Woodham Ferrers:**
Benfleet: SS7 . . . . .Ben	**Foulness Island:** SS3 . . . . .Fou I	**North Benfleet:** SS12 . . . . .Nth B	CM3 . . . . .Sth F
Bicknacre: CM3 . . . . .B'acre	**Hadleigh:** SS6-7 . . . . .Hadl'gh	**Orsett:** SS17 . . . . .Ors	**Stambridge:** SS4 . . . . .Stam
Billericay: CM4,CM11-13 . . . . . . .Bill	**Hawkwell:** SS5 . . . . .Hawk	**Pitsea:** SS7,SS13-14,SS16 . . . . . . .Pit	**Stanford-le-Hope:** SS17 . . . . . .Stan H
Bowers Gifford: SS13 . . . . .B Gif	**Hockley:** SS5 . . . . .Hock	**Ramsden Bellhouse:** CM11 . . . . .Ram	**Stock:** CM4 . . . . .Stock
Bulphan: RM14 . . . . .Bulp	**Horndon-on-the-Hill:**	**Ramsden Heath:** CM11 . . . . . .Ram H	**Stow Maries:** CM3 . . . . .Stow M
Burnham-on-Crouch: CM0 . . . .Bur C	SS16-17 . . . . .Horn H	**Rawreth:** SS11 . . . . .Raw	**Thundersley:** SS6-7 . . . . .Thun
Canewdon: SS4 . . . . .Cwdn	**Hullbridge:** SS5 . . . . .Hull	**Rayleigh:** SS5-7,SS9,SS11 . . . . . . .Ray	**Vange:** SS16-17 . . . . .Vange
Canvey Island: SS7-9 . . . . .Can I	**Hutton:** CM13 . . . . .Hut	**Rettendon:** CM3,SS11 . . . . .Ret	**Westcliff-on-Sea:** SS0,SS9 . . . .Wclf S
Corringham: SS17 . . . . .Corr	**Laindon:** SS14-15 . . . . .Lain	**Rochford:** SS4 . . . . .R'fd	**Wickford:** SS11-12 . . . . .Wick
Coryton: SS17 . . . . .Cory		**Runwell:** SS11 . . . . .Runw	**Woodham Ferrers:** CM3 . . . . . .Wdhm F

A

	Acorn Pl. SS16: Lan H 7D **14**	**Albany Av.** SS0: Wclf S 4C **32**	**Alderwood Way** SS7: Hadl'gh 2J **29**
	Acorns SS8: Can I 4J **39**	**Albany Ri.** SS6: Ray 3B **20**	**Aldham Gdns.** SS6: Ray 1F **19**
	Acorns, The SS5: Hock 4E **12**	**Albany Rd.** SS6: Ray 3C **20**	**Aldria Rd.** SS17: Stan H 2E **36**
	Acres, The SS17: Stan H 4F **37**	SS12: Wick 5F **9**	**Aldrin Cl.** SS17: Stan H 5E **36**
	Adalia Cres. SS9: Lgh S 2D **30**	**Albert Cl.** SS4: Ashin 5J **13**	**Aldrin Way** SS9: Lgh S 6J **21**
Aalten Av. SS8: Can I 5K **39**	**Adalia Way** SS9: Lgh S 3D **30**	SS6: Ray 1B **20**	**Alexander M.** CM12: Bill 5F **5**
Aaron Lewis Cl. SS5: Hawk 7F **13**	**Adams Bus. Cen.** SS14: Bas 3C **16**	**Albert Ct.** SS15: Lain 6E **14**	**Alexander Rd.** SS16: Lan H 2D **24**
Abbey Cl. SS5: Hull 1H **11**	**Adalia Way** SS9: Lgh S 3G **31**	**Albert M.** SS0: Wclf S 5C **32**	**Alexandra Ct.** SS1: Sth S 6D **32**
Abbeyfield Ho. SS7: Hadl'gh 2J **29**	**Adams Glade** SS4: Ashin 5K **13**	**Albert Pl.** *SS1: Sth S* *6G 33*	SS2: Sth S 4D **32**
Abbey Path SS15: Lain 5F **15**	**Adams Rd.** SS17: Stan H 6E **36**	(off Beach Rd.)	**Alexandra Hgts.** SS1: Sth S 4A **34**
Abbey Rd. CM12: Bill 6D **4**	**Adamsley Rd.** SS17: Stan H 7B **36**	**Albert Rd.** CM0: Bur C 6D **40**	**Alexandra Rd.** CM0: Bur C 5C **40**
SS5: Hull 2H **11**	**Adams Rd.** SS11: Wick 3G **9**	CM3: Sth F 3G **7**	SS1: Sth S 6D **32**
Abbots Ct. SS15: Bas 3G **15**	**Adelaide Gdns.** SS7: Ben 4D **28**	SS1: Sth S 3A **34**	SS3: Gt W 2F **35**
Abbotsleigh Rd. CM3: Sth F 4H **7**	**Adelsburg Rd.** SS8: Can I 4G **39**	(Armitage Rd.)	SS4: Ashin 5J **13**
Abbots Ride CM11: Bill 5G **5**	**Admirals Pl.** SS0: Wclf S 6A **32**	SS1: Sth S 6F **33**	SS6: Ray 1A **20**
Abbots Wlk. SS3: Shoe 4C **34**	**Admirals Wlk.** SS3: Shoe 6D **34**	(Stanley Rd.)	SS7: Ben 3D **28**
Abbotswood SS7: Thun 7J **19**	**Adventure Island**	SS4: Ashin 5J **13**	SS9: Lgh S 5G **31**
Abbotts Cl. SS9: Lgh S 7G **21**	Southend-on-Sea 6F **33**	SS6: Ray 1B **20**	**Alexandra St.** SS1: Sth S 6E **32**
Abbotts Dr. SS17: Stan H 5D **36**	**Afflets Ct.** SS14: Bas 4A **16**	SS7: Thun 6B **18**	**Alexandra Yacht Club** 6E **32**
Abbotts Hall Chase	**Agnes Av.** SS9: Lgh S 3D **30**	**Albion Ct.** CM12: Bill 6E **4**	**Alexandra Way** SS6: Ray 7E **10**
SS17: Stan H 5E **36**	**Ailsa Rd.** SS0: Wclf S 5A **32**	**Albion Rd.** SS0: Wclf S 4C **32**	**Aldria Rd.** SS17: Stan H 1B 20
Abensburg Rd. SS8: Can I 3H **39**	**Airborne Cl.** SS9: Lgh S 7G **21**	SS7: Ben 1C **28**	**Alfreda Av.** SS5: Hull 7H **7**
Aberdeen Gdns. SS9: Lgh S 3C **30**	**Airborne Cl.** CM3: Sth F 3J **7**	**Albyns** SS16: Lan H 1E **24**	**Alfred Gdns.** SS11: Wick 2F **9**
Abingdon Cl. SS15: Lain 4C **14**	**Akenfield Cl.** CM3: Sth F 3J **7**	**Alcotes** SS14: Bas 7D **16**	**Algars Way** CM3: Sth F 2H **7**
Abingdon Ct. SS13: Bas 3E **16**	**Alan Cl.** SS9: Lgh S 6G **21**	**Alder Cl.** SS15: Lain 3F **15**	**Alicia Av.** SS11: Wick 4J **9**
Abrahams Cl. SS14: Bas 3E **16**	**Alan Gro.** SS9: Lgh S 6G **21**	**Alderleys** SS7: Thun 6G **19**	**Alicia Cl.** SS11: Wick 4J **9**
Abrahams Way SS14: Bas 3E **16**		**Aldermans Hill** SS5: Hock 6B **12**	**Alicia Wlk.** SS11: Wick 3J **9**
Abreys SS7: Thun 5G **19**	**Airborne Cl.** SS9: Lgh S 7G **21**	**Alderman Wlk.** SS17: Stan H 2E **36**	**Alicia Way** SS11: Wick 4J **9**
Acacia Dr. SS15: Lain 4A **34**	**Akenfield Cl.** CM3: Sth F 3J **7**	**Alderney Gdns.** SS11: Wick 1E **8**	**Allandale** SS7: Thun 5G **19**
Acacia Rd. SS13: B Gif 4J **17**	**Alan Cl.** SS9: Lgh S 6G **21**		**Allensway** SS17: Stan H 4F **37**
Academy Dr. SS15: Lain 4D **14**	**Alan Gro.** SS9: Lgh S 6G **21**		

Allerton Cl.—Beaver Twr.

Allerton Cl. SS4: Ashin 5J **13**
Alley Dock SS9: Can I, Lgh S 5F **31**
Alleyn Pl. SS0: Wclf S 4B **32**
Allington Ct. CM11: Bill 6A **4**
Allistonway SS17: Stan H 4F **37**
Allysum Wlk. CM12: Bill 2D **4**
Alma Cl. SS7: Hadl'gh 3B **30**
SS12: Wick 5C **8**
Alma Link CM12: Bill 5E **4**
Alma Rd. SS7: Hadl'gh 3C **30**
Almere SS7: Ben 1D **28**
Almond Av. SS5: Hull 6J **7**
SS12: Wick 4E **8**
Almond Wlk. SS8: Can I 4D **38**
Alnwick Cl. SS16: Lan H 7B **14**
Alp Ct. SS3: Gt W 1G **35**
Alpha Cl. SS13: B Gif 6K **17**
Alpha Rd. CM0: Bur C 5D **40**
SS13: B Gif 6K **17**
Alracks SS15: Lain 6G **15**
Alresford Grn. SS12: Wick 5G **9**
Alston Ct. SS0: Wclf S 4A **32**
Altar Pl. SS15: Lain 5E **14**
Althorne Cl. SS13: Bas 3F **17**
Althorpe Cl. SS5: Hock 5D **12**
Alton Gdns. SS2: Sth S 7C **22**
Amberden SS15: Lain 7F **15**
Ambleside Dr. SS1: Sth S 5G **33**
Ambleside Gdns. SS5: Hull 1H **11**
Ambleside Wlk. SS8: Can I 4D **38**
Ambrose Chase SS14: Bas 6J **15**
Ameland Rd. SS8: Can I 2E **38**
Amelia Blackwell Ho.
SS8: Can I 5C **38**
Amersham Av. SS16: Lan H 7B **14**
Amid Rd. SS8: Can I 3G **39**
Ampers End SS14: Bas 7B **16**
Anchorage *SS8: Can I 7F 39*
(off Western Esplanade)
Anchorage, The CM0: Bur C 7D **40**
SS3: Gt W 1H **35**
Anchor Cl. SS3: Shoe 6F **35**
Anchor Reach CM3: Sth F 5J **7**
Anders Fall SS9: Lgh S 6J **21**
Andersons SS17: Stan H 4F **37**
Andersons Ind. Est.
SS12: Wick 7F **9**
Andrew Cl. SS17: Stan H 3D **36**
Andyk Rd. SS8: Can I 5J **39**
Anerley Rd. SS0: Wclf S 5B **32**
Angel Cl. SS16: Vange 2B **26**
Anglesey Gdns. SS12: Wick 6H **9**
Anne Boleyn Dr. SS4: R'fd 5D **22**
Anne Boleyn Mans. SS13: Pit . . .7F **17**
Annett Cl. SS12: Wick 6J **9**
Annwood Lodge Bus. Pk.
SS6: Ray 2D **18**
Anson Chase SS3: Shoe 4E **34**
Anson Cl. CM3: Sth F 4K **7**
Anstey Cl. SS9: Lgh S 5F **21**
Anthony Cl. CM11: Bill 7B **4**
Anthony Dr. SS17: Stan H 3E **36**
Antlers SS8: Can I 6D **38**
Antony Cl. SS8: Can I 3F **39**
Antrim Rd. SS3: Shoe 5D **34**
Anvil Way CM12: Bill 2F **5**
Apeldoorn SS7: Thun 5B **18**
Apollo Dr. SS2: Sth S 5J **33**
Appleby Dr. SS16: Lan H 7B **14**
Appledene Cl. SS6: Ray 7H **11**
Appledore SS3: Shoe 3C **34**
Appleford Ct. SS13: Pit 6G **17**
Applerow SS9: Lgh S 6H **21**
Appleton Rd. SS7: Ben 2B **28**
Appletree Cl. SS2: Sth S 2J **33**
Appletree Way SS11: Wick 3H **9**
Appleyard Av. SS5: Hock 3E **12**
Approach, The SS6: Ray 1J **19**
Approach Rd. SS8: Can I 5K **39**
Aragon Cl. SS2: Sth S 1C **32**
Aragon Ct. SS7: Hadl'gh 3B **30**
SS13: Pit 1F 27
(off Station La.)
Arcade, The SS11: Wick 3F **9**
Arcadian Gdns. SS7: Hadl'gh 1J **29**
Arcadia Rd. CM0: Bur C 5D **40**
SS8: Can I 5H **39**
Archer Av. SS2: Sth S 2H **33**
Archer Cl. SS2: Sth S 2J **33**
Archer Rd. SS15: Lain 4D **14**
Archers Cl. CM12: Bill 7E **4**
Archers Flds. SS13: Bas 3F **17**
Archers Flds. Cl. SS13: Bas 3E **16**
Archibald Ter. SS15: Lain 5D **14**
Ardleigh SS16: Bas 7G **15**
Ardley Way SS6: Ray 7H **11**
Argent Ct. SS15: Lain 5B **14**
Argyle Rd. CM0: Bur C 6E **40**
Argyll Ho. SS0: Wclf S 6B **32**
Argyll Rd. SS0: Wclf S 5B **32**
Arjan Way SS8: Can I 5A **38**
Ark La. SS4: R'fd 3H **21**
Arlington Rd. SS2: Sth S 4J **33**
Arlington Sq. CM3: Sth F 5G **7**
Arlington Way CM12: Bill 2D **4**
Armada Cl. SS15: Lain 7F **15**
Armadale SS8: Can I 3D **38**
Armagh Rd. SS3: Shoe 5D **34**
Armath Pl. SS16: Lan H 1B **24**
Armitage Rd. SS1: Sth S 3A **34**
Armstrong Cl. SS17: Stan H 5E **36**
Armstrong Rd. SS7: Thun 5D **18**
Arne Cl. SS17: Stan H 4D **36**
Arne Ct. SS15: Lain 4E **14**
Arne M. SS15: Lain 4E **14**
Arnheim Rd. CM0: Bur C 6D **40**
Arnold Av. SS1: Sth S 6G **33**
SS16: Lan H 7C **14**
Arnold Cen., The SS14: Bas 2D **16**
Arnolds Way SS4: Ashin 4K **13**
Arran Ct. SS12: Wick 5H **9**
Arterial Rd. SS17: Stan H 4C **36**
Artillery Av. SS3: Shoe 4D **34**
Arundel Cl. CM12: Bill 1G **5**
Arundel Dr. SS17: Corr 3G **37**
Arundel Gdns. SS0: Wclf S 2J **31**
SS6: Ray 6F **11**
Arundel M. CM12: Bill 1G **5**
Arundel Rd. SS4: Ashin 2J **13**
SS7: Thun 5B **18**
SS11: Wick 2E **8**
Arundel Way CM12: Bill 1G **5**
Arwen Gro. CM3: Sth F 4G **7**
Ascot Cl. SS7: Thun 5H **19**
Ascot Gro. SS14: Bas 6D **16**
Ascot M. CM0: S'min 5H **41**
Ashanti Cl. SS3: Shoe 4F **35**
Ash Av. SS9: Lgh S 6D **20**
Ashbrook Pl. SS6: Ray 4B **20**
Ashburnham Rd. SS1: Sth S 5D **32**
Ashcombe SS4: R'fd 1B **22**
Ashcombe Cl. SS9: Lgh S 6D **20**
Ashcombe Way SS6: Ray 2B **20**
Ash Ct. SS3: Shoe 6F **35**
Ashdene Cl. SS5: Hull 1J **11**
Ashdon Way SS16: Bas 7J **15**
Ashdown Cl. SS17: Corr 2F **37**
Ashdown Cres. SS7: Hadl'gh 1A **30**
Ashdown Ho. *SS7: Thun 6F 19*
(off Avington Wlk.)
ASHELDHAM **2K 41**
Ashes Rd. SS3: Shoe 6E **34**
Ashfield SS6: Ray 1F **19**
Ashfields SS13: Pit 5G **17**
Ash Grn. CM11: Bill 5H **5**
Ash Gro. CM0: Bur C 4C **40**
Ashingdale Cl. SS8: Can I 6F **39**
ASHINGDON **6K 13**
Ashingdon Hgts. SS4: Ashin 4H **13**
Ashingdon Rd.
SS4: Ashin, R'fd 2H **13**
Ashleigh Cl. SS8: Can I 2E **38**
Ashleigh Ct. SS8: Can I 2E **38**
Ashleigh Dr. SS9: Lgh S 5H **31**
Ashley Cl. SS17: Corr 3G **37**
Ashlyns SS13: Pit 5E **16**
Ashmans Row CM3: Sth F 4H **7**
Ash Rd. SS7: Hadl'gh 3A **30**
SS8: Can I 5G **39**
Ash Tree Wlk. SS14: Bas 7D **16**
Ashurst Av. SS2: Sth S 4K **33**
Ash Wlk. SS1: Sth S 6F **33**
Ash Way SS5: Hock 3E **12**
Ashway SS17: Corr 2H **37**
Ashwood SS7: Thun 5B **18**
Ashwood Cl. CM0: Bur C 3C **40**
Ashworths SS4: Ashin 5J **13**
SS8: Can I 2E **38**
Aspect Arena, The **7D 38**
Aspen Cl. SS8: Can I 4C **38**
Aspen Ct. SS15: Lain 3E **14**
Aspen Gro. SS4: Ashin 4J **13**
Asquith Av. SS7: Thun 6H **19**
Asquith Gdns. SS7: Thun 5J **19**
Assandune Cl. SS4: Ashin 4K **13**
Aster Cl. SS15: Lain 7F **15**
Aston Rd. SS15: Lain 6D **14**
Astors, The SS5: Hock 5B **12**
Athelstan Gdns. SS11: Wick 2F **9**
(Hereward Gdns.)
SS11: Wick 2H **9**
(Whist Av.)
Athena Cl. SS2: Sth S 5J **33**
Atherstone Cl. SS8: Can I 6G **39**
Atherstone Rd. SS8: Can I 6G **39**
Athol Cl. SS8: Can I 6K **39**
Athos Rd. SS8: Can I 3G **39**
Atridge Chase CM12: Bill 3E **4**
Audley Ct. SS1: Sth S 7G **33**
Audleys Cl. SS2: Sth S 7C **22**
Audley Way SS14: Bas 6J **15**
Augusta Rd. SS17: Stan H 7B **36**
Aurum Ct. SS15: Lain 5B **14**
Austen Rd. SS14: Bas 5D **16**
Autumn M. SS15: Lain 3E **14**
Avebury Rd. SS0: Wclf S 4C **32**
Avenue, The CM12: Bill 5D **4**
SS5: Hull 7H **7**
SS7: Hadl'gh 2A **30**
SS8: Can I 6F **39**
SS17: Fob 2K **37**
Avenue Rd. SS0: Wclf S 5D **32**
SS7: Ben 2E **28**
SS9: Lgh S 5G **31**
Avenue Ter. SS0: Wclf S 5C **32**
Aviation Way SS2: Sth S 5K **21**
Aviation Way Ind. Area
SS2: Sth S 5K **21**
Avington Wlk. SS7: Thun 6F **19**
Avoca Ter. *SS0: Wclf S 3B 32*
(off Fairfax Dr.)
Avon Cl. SS4: Ashin 6J **13**
Avondale Cl. SS6: Ray 2B **20**
Avondale Dr. SS9: Lgh S 1H **31**
Avondale Gdns.
SS17: Stan H 2E **36**
Avondale Rd. SS6: Ray 2B **20**
SS7: Ben 2D **28**
SS16: Vange 1E **26**
Avondale Wlk. SS8: Can I 4C **38**
Avon Rd. SS8: Can I 5E **38**
Avon Way SS3: Shoe 5D **34**
SS14: Bas 5D **16**
Avro Rd. SS2: Sth S 6B **22**
Axis Ct. SS1: Sth S 5F **33**
Aydon Cl. SS11: Wick 2E **8**
Aylesbeare SS3: Shoe 4D **34**
Aylesbury Dr. SS16: Lan H 7B **14**
Aylesbury M. SS15: Bas 2H **15**
Aylett Cl. SS8: Can I 4G **39**
Ayletts SS14: Bas 6D **16**
Azalea Av. SS12: Wick 4E **8**
Azalea M. SS8: Can I 6E **38**

B

Baardwyk Av. SS8: Can I 5J **39**
Back La. SS4: R'fd 3D **22**
Badger Hall Av. SS7: Thun 1G **29**
Badgers, The SS16: Lan H 1C **24**
Badgers Cl. SS0: Wclf S 1K **31**
Badgers Keep CM0: Bur C 2C **40**
Badgers Mt. SS5: Hock 6C **12**
Badgers Wlk. SS5: Hawk 1H **21**
Badgers Way SS7: Thun 1G **29**
Badnocks Chase CM0: Ashel 1G **41**
Bailey, The SS6: Ray 2J **19**
Bailey Rd. SS9: Lgh S 3D **30**
Baker Cl. SS15: Lain 7E **14**
Bakers Cl. CM3: Sth F 2H **7**
Bakers Ct. SS14: Bas 2E **16**
Bakers Farm Cl. SS11: Wick 4J **9**
Balfour Cl. SS12: Wick 6G **9**
Ballards Wlk. SS15: Lain 5G **15**
Balmerino Av. SS7: Thun 6J **19**
Balmoral Av. SS17: Corr 3G **37**
SS17: Stan H 4E **36**
Balmoral Cl. CM11: Bill 6J **5**
Balmoral Gdns. SS5: Hock 5C **12**
Balmoral Ho. SS0: Wclf S 5C **32**
Balmoral Rd. SS0: Wclf S 5C **32**
Balmoral Ter. *SS0: Wclf S 3B 32*
(off Fairfax Dr.)
BALSTONIA **3F 37**
Balstonia Dr. SS17: Stan H 2E **36**
Baltic Av. SS1: Sth S 5E **32**
Bancrofts Rd. CM3: Sth F 2J **7**
Bandhills Cl. CM3: Sth F 2H **7**
Bankside Cl. CM3: Sth F 1J **7**
Bannister Grn. SS12: Wick 5G **9**
Banyard Way SS4: R'fd 7J **13**
Barbara Av. SS8: Can I 5D **38**
Barbara Cl. SS4: R'fd 2C **22**
Barbour Grn. SS12: Wick 6F **9**
Barclay Rd. SS13: B Gif 3J **17**
Bardenville Rd. SS8: Can I 5J **39**
Bardfield SS16: Vange 7C **16**
Bardfield Way SS6: Ray 1G **19**
Barge Pier Rd. SS3: Shoe 7E **34**
Barley Cl. SS16: Lan H 2C **24**
Barleylands Rd. CM11: Bill 1H **15**
SS15: Bas 1H **15**
Barling Rd.
SS3: Barl M, Gt W
. . . . .1A **34**, 1K **33**
Barnaby Way SS15: Lain 5F **15**
Barnard Cl. SS16: Vange 3C **26**
Barnard Rd. SS9: Lgh S 3D **30**
Barnards Av. SS8: Can I 4H **39**
Barncombe Cl. SS7: Thun 6D **18**
Barnet Pk. Rd. SS11: Runw 1H **9**
Barneveld Av. SS8: Can I 5J **39**
Barnfield SS11: Wick 3G **9**
Barn Hall Cotts. SS11: Wick 1D **8**
Barnmead Way CM0: Bur C 3C **40**
Barnstaple Cl. SS1: Sth S 4A **34**
Barnstaple Rd. SS1: Sth S 4A **34**
Barnwell Dr. SS5: Hock 5D **12**
Barnyard, The SS16: Lan H 1C **24**
Baron Ct. SS2: Sth S 7D **22**
Baron Rd. CM3: Sth F 3J **7**
Barons Ct. Rd. SS6: Ray 5G **11**
Barons Way SS16: Lan H 1D **24**
Barra Glade SS12: Wick 6H **9**
Barrie Pavement SS12: Wick 6F **9**
Barrington Cl. SS3: Shoe 3E **34**
SS14: Bas 4D **16**
Barrington Gdns. SS14: Bas 4D **16**
Barringtons Cl. SS6: Ray 1K **19**
Barrowsand SS1: Sth S 6B **34**
Barrymore Wlk. SS6: Ray 2B **20**
BARSTABLE **6C 16**
Barstable Rd. SS17: Stan H 5D **36**
Bartletts SS6: Ray 4C **20**
Bartley Cl. SS7: Thun 6B **18**
Bartley Rd. SS7: Thun 6B **18**
Bartlow End SS13: Bas 4F **17**
Bartlow Side SS13: Bas 4F **17**
Barton Cl. CM3: Sth F 1H **7**
Baryta Cl. SS17: Stan H 6C **36**
Baryta Ct. *SS9: Lgh S 4G 31*
(off Rectory Gro.)
BASILDON **7J 15**
Basildon & District Crematorium
SS13: B Gif 1J **27**
Basildon Bowl **6J 15**
Basildon Bus. Cen. SS14: Bas . . .4J **15**
Basildon Bus Station **7J 15**
Basildon Cen., The
SS14: Bas 6J **15**
Basildon Dr. SS15: Lain 5E **14**
Basildon Golf Course **2K 25**
Basildon Ri. SS15: Lain 4G **15**
Basildon Rd. SS15: Lain 4G **15**
Basildon Sporting Village **5H 15**
Basildon Sports Cen. **2H 25**
Basildon Station (Rail) **7J 15**
Basildon Trad. Cen.
SS14: Bas 4H **15**
BASILDON UNIVERSITY HOSPITAL
. . . .**2H 25**
Bassenthwaite Rd. SS7: Thun . . .6E **18**
Batavia Rd. SS8: Can I 4B **38**
BATTLESBRIDGE **1B 10**
Battlesbridge Antiques Cen. . . .**1B 10**
Battlesbridge Harbour
SS11: Bat 1C **10**
Battlesbridge Station (Rail) **1B 10**
Battleswick SS14: Bas 3C **16**
Baxter Av. SS2: Sth S 4D **32**
Bay Cl. SS8: Can I 6F **39**
Beach Av. SS9: Lgh S 4J **31**
Beach Ct. SS0: Wclf S 6A **32**
SS3: Gt W 1J **35**
Beaches Cl. SS5: Hock 5G **13**
Beach Ho. Gdns. SS8: Can I 6J **39**
Beach Rd. SS1: Sth S 6G **33**
SS3: Shoe 7F **35**
SS8: Can I 4H **39**
Beachway SS8: Can I 6F **39**
Beambridge SS13: Pit 6E **16**
Beambridge Ct. SS13: Pit 6E **16**
Beambridge M. SS13: Pit 6E **16**
Beambridge Pl. SS13: Pit 6E **16**
Beams Cl. CM11: Bill 7G **5**
Beams Way CM11: Bill 7G **5**
Bearsted Dr. SS13: Pit 7G **17**
Bearwood Rd. SS17: Stan H 7B **36**
Beatrice Av. SS8: Can I 4F **39**
Beatrice Cl. SS5: Hock 5D **12**
Beatty La. SS14: Bas 6C **16**
Beatty Ri. CM3: Sth F 4K **7**
Beauchamps CM0: Bur C 2C **40**
Beauchamps Dr. SS11: Wick 4H **9**
Beaufort Rd. CM12: Bill 5D **4**
Beaufort St. SS2: Sth S 4H **33**
Beaver Twr. SS9: Lgh S 6G **21**

Cassel Av.—Clavering Ct.

Cassel Av. SS8: Can I 3G **39**
Castle Av. SS7: Hadl'gh 4K **29**
Castle Cl. SS3: Shoe 4G **35**
SS6: Ray 3J **19**
Castle Ct. SS6: Ray 3J **19**
SS7: Hadl'gh 3A **30**
Castledon Rd. CM11: D'ham 1C **8**
SS12: Wick 1C **8**
Castle Dr. SS6: Ray 1J **19**
SS9: Lgh S 5D **30**
Castle La. SS7: Hadl'gh 4K **29**
Castle Point Athletics Track 2B 38
Castle Point Golf Course 2D 38
Castle Rd. SS6: Ray 3J **19**
SS7: Hadl'gh 3K **29**
Castle Ter. SS6: Ray 2J **19**
Castleton Rd. SS2: Sth S 4J **33**
Castle Vw. Rd. SS8: Can I 2E **38**
Castle Wlk. SS8: Can I 3E **38**
SS13: Pit 6G **17**
Caswell Cl. SS17: Corr 3G **37**
Cater Mus. . . . . **.5E 4**
Caterwood CM12: Bill 4F **5**
Cathedral Dr. SS15: Lain 5E **14**
Catherine Lodge SS2: Sth S 4D **32**
Catherine Rd. SS7: Ben 1D **28**
Cattawade End SS14: Bas 5B **16**
Cattawade Link SS14: Bas 5B **16**
Caulfield Rd. SS3: Shoe 6C **34**
Causton Way SS6: Ray 7H **11**
Cavell Ct. *SS14: Bas 5C* ***16***
(off Nightingale Gro.)
Cavell Rd. CM11: Bill 6G **5**
Cavendish Ct. *SS16: Bas 7J* ***15***
(off Bessemer Cl.)
Cavendish Gdns. SS0: Wclf S . . .3J **31**
Cavendish Rd. SS5: Hock 2F **13**
Cavendish Way SS15: Lain 3F **15**
Caversham Av. SS3: Shoe 2E **34**
Caversham Pk. Av. SS6: Ray 7G **11**
(Downhall Pk. Way)
SS6: Ray 6G **11**
(Manns Way)
Cecil Ct. SS2: Sth S 2C **32**
Cecil Dr. SS13: Pit 4H **17**
Cecil Way SS6: Ray 2B **20**
Cedar Av. SS12: Wick 6E **8**
Cedar Cl. SS2: Sth S 3E **32**
SS6: Ray 3B **20**
Cedar Ct. SS3: Shoe 5E **34**
Cedar Dr. SS5: Hull 1J **11**
Cedar Gro. CM0: Bur C 4C **40**
Cedar Hall Gdns. SS7: Thun 6G **19**
Cedar M. SS5: Hock 5C **12**
Cedar Pk. Cl. SS7: Thun 6G **19**
Cedar Rd. SS7: Thun 6G **19**
SS8: Can I 4D **38**
Cedars SS17: Stan H 5E **36**
Cedars, The CM3: Sth F 2H **7**
SS3: Gt W 1H **35**
Celandine Cl. CM12: Bill 3D **4**
Celeborn St. CM3: Sth F 4F **7**
Central Av. CM12: Bill 2G **5**
SS2: Sth S 4F **33**
SS4: Ashin 6J **13**
SS5: Hull 3K **11**
SS7: Hadl'gh 7A **20**
SS8: Can I 4C **38**
SS16: Lan H 1A **24**
SS17: Corr 3G **37**
SS17: Stan H 2E **36**
Central Cl. SS7: Hadl'gh 1A **30**
Central Rd. SS17: Stan H 6D **36**
Central Wall SS8: Can I 2D **38**
(not continuous)
Central Wall Cotts. SS8: Can I . . .3F **39**
Central Wall Rd. SS8: Can I 3F **39**
Centre Pl. *SS1: Sth S 6G* ***33***
(off Prospect Cl.)
Centre Reach *SS2: Sth S 4E* ***32***
(off Coleman St.)
Centurion Cl. SS3: Shoe 4F **35**
Ceylon Rd. SS0: Wclf S 5B **32**
Chadacre Rd. SS1: Sth S 3B **34**
Chadwick Ct. SS0: Wclf S 5A **32**
Chadwick Rd. CM3: Sth F 1J **7**
SS0: Wclf S 5A **32**
Chaffinch Cl. SS3: Shoe 4E **34**
Chaffinch Cres. CM11: Bill 6G **5**
Chaingate Av. SS2: Sth S 3J **33**
Chale Ct. SS17: Stan H 7C **36**
Chalfont Cl. SS9: Lgh S 1F **31**
Chalice Cl. SS14: Bas 6C **16**
Chalk End SS13: Pit 6E **16**
Chalk Rd. SS8: Can I 2E **38**
CHALKWELL 5J 31
Chalkwell Av. SS0: Wclf S 6K **31**
Chalkwell Bay SS9: Lgh S 5J **31**
Chalkwell Esplanade
SS0: Wclf S 5J **31**
Chalkwell Lodge SS0: Wclf S . . .4A **32**
Chalkwell Pk. Dr. SS9: Lgh S . . .4H **31**
Chalkwell Station (Rail) 5J 31
Challacombe SS1: Sth S 3C **34**
Challock Lees SS13: Pit 7G **17**
CHALVEDON 6F 17
Chalvedon Av. SS13: Pit 5F **17**
Chalvedon Sq. SS13: Pit 6E **16**
Chamberlain Av. SS8: Can I 4G **39**
SS17: Corr 2G **37**
Chamberlains Ride CM3: Sth F . . .5H **7**
Champion Cl. SS12: Wick 5F **9**
SS17: Stan H 4E **36**
Champions Way CM3: Sth F 2G **7**
Champlain Av. SS8: Can I 3D **38**
Chancel Cl. SS7: Thun 6C **18**
SS15: Lain 5E **14**
Chancellor Rd. SS1: Sth S 6F **33**
Chandlers CM0: Bur C 4B **40**
Chandlers Chase CM12: Bill 5E **4**
Chandlers Way CM3: Sth F 3J **7**
SS2: Sth S 7D **22**
Chandos Pde. SS7: Hadl'gh 2B **30**
Chanton Cl. SS9: Lgh S 5F **21**
Chantry Chase CM11: Bill 5F **5**
Chantry Cres. SS17: Stan H 6C **36**
Chantry La. SS15: Lain 5E **14**
Chantry Way CM11: Bill 5F **5**
Chapel Ct. CM12: Bill 5F **5**
Chapel La. SS3: Gt W 1H **35**
SS7: Hadl'gh 3J **29**
Chapel M. CM12: Bill 6F **5**
Chapel Pl. SS3: Shoe 6F **35**
Chapel Rd. CM0: Bur C 6D **40**
SS3: Shoe 6F **35**
Chapel St. CM12: Bill 5E **4**
Chaplin Cl. SS15: Bas 3G **15**
Chapman Ct. SS6: Ray 6H **11**
SS8: Can I 6J **39**
Chapman Rd. SS8: Can I 5K **39**
Chapman Sands Sailing Club . . .6J 39
Chapmans Cl. SS9: Lgh S 4D **30**
Chapmans Wlk. SS9: Lgh S 4D **30**
Charfleets Cl. SS8: Can I 5B **38**
Charfleets Farm Ind. Est.
SS8: Can I 5B **38**
Charfleets Farm Way
SS8: Can I 5B **38**
Charfleets Ind. Est.
SS8: Can I 5A **38**
Charfleets Rd. SS8: Can I 5A **38**
Charfleets Service Rd.
SS8: Can I 5B **38**
Charity Farm Chase CM12: Bill . . .4D **4**
Charles Cl. SS0: Wclf S 7J **21**
Charleston Av. SS13: Bas 3G **17**
Charleston Ct. SS13: Bas 3G **17**
Charlotte Av. SS12: Wick 3E **8**
Charlotte Ct. CM3: Sth F 4H **7**
Charlotte M. SS2: Sth S 4D **32**
Charlton Cl. SS13: Pit 5G **17**
Charnwood Wlk. SS7: Hadl'gh . . .1A **30**
Charterhouse SS16: Vange 7A **16**
Charters Ct. SS11: Wick 3H **9**
Chartwell Nth. *SS2: Sth S 5E* ***32***
(within Victoria Plaza Shop. Cen.)
CHARTWELL PRIVATE HOSPITAL
. . . . .3D 30
Chartwell Sq. *SS2: Sth S 5E* ***32***
(within Victoria Plaza Shop. Cen.)
Chartwell W. *SS2: Sth S 5E* ***32***
(within Victoria Plaza Shop. Cen.)
Chase, The CM0: S'min 5G **41**
CM3: Sth F 2G **7**
CM11: Bill 5G **5**
CM12: Bas, L Bur 2D **14**
SS4: Ashin 4H **13**
SS6: Ray 3B **20**
SS7: Thun 7F **19**
SS12: Wick 7G **9**
(The Crossway)
SS12: Wick 4C **8**
(Tudor Way)
SS16: Bas 2G **25**
Chase Cl. SS7: Thun 7F **19**
Chase Ct. Gdns. *SS1: Sth S 5G* ***33***
(off Chase Rd.)
Chase Dr. CM3: Sth F 2G **7**
Chase End SS6: Ray 2B **20**
Chase Gdns. SS0: Wclf S 2B **32**
Chase Rd. SS1: Sth S 5G **33**
SS17: Corr 4G **37**
Chaseside SS6: Ray 4A **20**
Chase Sports & Fitness Cen. . . .2A 32
Chaseway SS16: Vange 1D **26**
Chaseway End SS16: Vange 2D **26**
Chatfield Way SS13: Pit 5G **17**
Chatham Pavement SS13: Pit . . .5G **17**
Chatsworth SS7: Thun 6F **19**
Chatsworth Gdns. SS5: Hock 5D **12**
Chatterford End SS14: Bas 5J **15**
Chatton Cl. SS12: Wick 6G **9**
Chaucer Ho. SS2: Sth S 3F **33**
Chaucer Wlk. SS12: Wick 6F **9**
Cheapside E. SS6: Ray 7G **11**
Cheapside W. SS6: Ray 7E **10**
Cheddar Av. SS0: Wclf S 7J **21**
Chedington SS3: Shoe 3C **34**
Cheldon Barton SS1: Sth S 3C **34**
Chelmer Av. SS6: Ray 3J **19**
Chelmer Way CM0: Bur C 4B **40**
SS3: Shoe 5D **34**
Chelmsford Av. SS2: Sth S 4D **32**
Chelmsford Rd. SS11: Raw 2C **10**
Chelsea Av. SS1: Sth S 7H **33**
Chelsea Ct. SS1: Sth S 5G **33**
SS4: R'fd 2C **22**
Chelsworth Cl. SS1: Sth S 5K **33**
Chelsworth Cres. SS1: Sth S 5J **33**
Cheltenham Dr. SS7: Thun 5H **19**
SS9: Lgh S 3H **31**
Cheltenham Rd. SS1: Sth S 5G **33**
SS5: Hock 4F **13**
Chenies Dr. SS15: Lain 3D **14**
Chepstow Cl. CM11: Bill 2H **5**
Cherries, The SS8: Can I 6F **39**
Cherrybrook SS1: Sth S 3C **34**
Cherry Cl. SS5: Hock 4E **12**
SS8: Can I 4C **38**
Cherry Ct. SS8: Can I 7F **39**
Cherrydene Cl. SS5: Hull 1J **11**
Cherrydown SS6: Ray 7H **11**
Cherrydown E. SS16: Bas 7J **15**
Cherrydown W. SS16: Bas 7J **15**
Cherry Gdns. CM12: Bill 3C **4**
Cherry La. SS11: Wick 4J **9**
Cherrymeade SS7: Thun 1G **29**
(not continuous)
Cherry Orchard CM0: S'min 5H **41**
Cherry Orchard Jubilee Country Pk.
. . . . .4G 21
Cherry Orchard La. SS4: R'fd . . .3K **21**
(not continuous)
Cherry Orchard Way
SS2: Sth S 3K **21**
SS4: R'fd 3K **21**
Cherrytree Chase SS3: Shoe 3J **35**
Cherry Trees CM12: Bill 7D **4**
Chertsey Cl. SS3: Shoe 3D **34**
Chesham Dr. SS15: Lain 3D **14**
Cheshunt Dr. SS6: Ray 5F **11**
Cheshunts SS13: Pit 6E **16**
Chester Av. SS1: Sth S 7H **33**
Chesterfield Av. SS7: Thun 6C **18**
Chesterfield Cres. SS9: Lgh S . . .6F **21**
Chesterford Gdns. SS14: Bas . . .4D **16**
Chesterford Grn. SS14: Bas 4D **16**
Chester Hall La. SS14: Bas 3J **15**
Chesterman Rd. SS3: Shoe 6F **35**
Chester Way SS14: Bas 4D **16**
Chestnut Av. CM12: Bill 5D **4**
Chestnut Cl. CM0: Bur C 5B **40**
SS5: Hock 5F **13**
Chestnut Ct. SS16: Vange 1E **26**
Chestnut Gro. SS2: Sth S 3E **32**
SS7: Ben 1B **28**
Chestnut Ho. SS11: Wick 4G **9**
Chestnut Rd. SS16: Vange 1E **26**
Chestnuts, The CM0: S'min 5G **41**
SS6: Ray 7K **11**
Chestnut Wlk. SS8: Can I 5C **38**
SS17: Corr 4H **37**
Chestwood Cl. CM12: Bill 2F **5**
Chevening Gdns. SS5: Hock 5C **12**
Chevers Pawen SS13: Pit 7E **16**
Cheviot Ho. SS2: Sth S 4D **32**
Cheviot Wlk. *SS2: Sth S 5E* ***32***
(within Victoria Plaza Shop. Cen.)
Cheyne Ct. SS12: Wick 7G **9**
Chichester Cl. SS8: Can I 6E **38**
SS14: Bas 5D **16**
Chichester Rd. SS1: Sth S 5E **32**
SS2: Sth S 5E **32**
Chignalls, The SS15: Lain 6C **14**
Chilham Cl. SS13: Pit 7G **17**
Chiltern *SS2: Sth S 5F* ***33***
(off Coleman St.)
Chiltern App. SS8: Can I 4C **38**
Chiltern Cl. SS6: Ray 1K **19**
Chilterns, The SS8: Can I 4D **38**
Chimes, The SS7: Ben 1E **28**
Chinchilla Rd. SS1: Sth S 5H **33**
Chipping Row CM3: Sth F 3J **7**
Chisholm Ct. SS12: Wick 6G **9**
Chittock Ga. SS14: Bas 6C **16**
Chittock Mead SS14: Bas 6C **16**
Chorley Cl. SS16: Lan H 7B **14**
Christchurch Av. SS12: Wick 3C **8**
Christchurch Ct. SS1: Sth S 5G **33**
Christchurch M. SS2: Sth S 4G **33**
Christchurch Rd. SS2: Sth S 4G **33**
Christmas Tree Cres.
SS5: Hawk 7G **13**
Christopher Martin Rd.
SS14: Bas 2C **16**
Christy Cl. SS15: Lain 5A **14**
Christy Ct. SS15: Lain 5A **14**
Christy Way SS15: Lain 5A **14**
Church Chase CM3: Ret 5A **6**
Church Cl. SS3: Shoe 6D **34**
SS8: Can I 5D **38**
SS17: Horn H 4A **36**
Church Cnr. SS7: Ben 4D **28**
Church Cotts. SS11: Runw 2G **9**
Church End Av. SS11: Runw 1G **9**
Church End La. SS11: Runw 1F **9**
Churchfields SS3: Shoe 2E **34**
Churchgate SS0: Wclf S 4A **32**
Church Hill SS9: Lgh S 5G **31**
SS13: Pit 1F **27**
SS15: Lain 5F **15**
SS17: Stan H 6C **36**
Churchill Av. SS14: Bas 5C **16**
Churchill Cres. SS17: Stan H 3E **36**
Churchill Sth. *SS2: Sth S 5E* ***32***
(within Victoria Plaza Shop. Cen.)
Churchill Sq. *SS2: Sth S 5E* ***32***
(within Victoria Plaza Shop. Cen.)
Churchill W. *SS2: Sth S 5E* ***32***
(within Victoria Plaza Shop. Cen.)
Church La. SS13: Bas 2E **16**
Church M. SS15: Lain 5D **14**
Church Pde. SS8: Can I 4C **38**
Church Pk. Rd. SS13: Pit 7F **17**
Church Path SS13: Pit 1F **27**
Church Rd. CM0: Bur C 4C **40**
CM11: Ram H 1A **8**
SS1: Sth S 6E **32**
SS3: Shoe 6C **34**
SS4: Ashin 4J **13**
SS5: Hock 2B **12**
SS6: Ray 2A **20**
SS7: Hadl'gh 2A **30**
SS7: Thun 6B **18**
SS11: Raw 4A **10**
SS13: B Gif 7H **17**
SS14: Bas 4A **16**
(not continuous)
SS15: Lain 3G **15**
(not continuous)
SS16: Vange 6A **16**
SS17: Corr 3H **37**
Church Rd. Res. Pk. Homes
SS17: Corr 4H **37**
Church St. CM11: Bill 7A **4**
SS6: Ray 2K **19**
Church Ter. *SS14: Bas 5A* ***16***
(off Church Rd.)
Church Vw. Cl. SS2: Sth S 3F **33**
Church Vw. Rd. SS7: Thun 6E **18**
Church Wlk. SS4: R'fd 3C **22**
SS14: Bas 6J **15**
Church Way SS7: Hadl'gh 3B **30**
Cimarron Cl. CM3: Sth F 3H **7**
Clara James Cotts. *SS8: Can I . . .5E* ***38***
(off Kitkatts Rd.)
Clare Av. SS11: Runw 1F **9**
Claremont Cl. SS0: Wclf S 4C **32**
Claremont Cres. SS6: Ray 7E **10**
Claremont Dr. SS16: Vange 1E **26**
Claremont Rd. SS0: Wclf S 4B **32**
SS15: Lain 4E **14**
Clarence Cl. SS7: Ben 1D **28**
Clarence Rd. SS1: Sth S 6E **32**
SS6: Ray 4B **20**
SS7: Ben 2D **28**
SS13: B Gif 5K **17**
SS17: Corr 3J **37**
Clarence Rd. Nth. SS7: Ben 1D **28**
Clarence St. SS1: Sth S 6E **32**
Clarendon Rd. SS5: Hock 2F **13**
SS8: Can I 4G **39**
SS13: Pit 5G **17**
Clare Rd. SS7: Thun 6A **18**
Claters Cl. SS2: Sth S 3K **33**
Clatterfield Gdns. SS0: Wclf S . . .3J **31**
Clavering SS16: Vange 1D **26**
Clavering Ct. SS6: Ray 1G **19**

Claybrick Av.—Cunningham Cl.

Claybrick Av. SS5: Hock ... 6D 12
Clayburn Circ. SS14: Bas ... 6B 16
Clayburn End SS14: Bas ... 6B 16
Clayburn Side SS14: Bas ... 6B 16
Claydon Cres. SS14: Bas ... 5A 16
Claydons La.
SS6: Hadl'gh, Ray ... 4J 19
SS7: Thun ... 5J 19
(Asquith Gdns.)
SS7: Thun ... 4J 19
(Rat La.)
Clay Hill La.
SS16: Bas, Vange ... 2K 25
Clay Hill Rd.
SS16: Bas, Vange ... 7K 15
Clayspring Cl. SS5: Hock ... 4D 12
Clayswell Ct. SS5: Hock ... 5E 12
Clements Gdns. SS5: Hawk ... 5G 13
Clements Grn. La.
CM3: Sth F ... 2H 7
Clements Hall SS5: Hawk ... 7G 13
Clements Hall La. SS5: Hawk ... 5G 13
Clements Hall Leisure Cen. ... 7G 13
Clements Pl. CM3: Sth F ... 2H 7
Clenshaw Path SS14: Bas ... 6J 15
Cleveden Ho. *SS7: Thun ... 6F 19*
(off Broadlands)
Cleveland Dr. SS0: Wclf S ... 2B 32
Cleveland Rd. SS8: Can I ... 6F 39
SS14: Bas ... 6A 16
Cleves Ct. SS7: Hadl'gh ... 2K 29
SS13: Pit ... 1F 27
(off Station La.)
Clevis Dr. CM3: Sth F ... 5K 7
Clickett End SS14: Bas ... 6A 16
Clickett Hill SS14: Bas ... 6A 16
Clickett Side SS14: Bas ... 6A 16
(not continuous)
Clieveden Rd. SS1: Sth S ... 7K 33
Cliff Av. SS0: Wclf S ... 4C 32
SS9: Lgh S ... 5J 31
Cliff Gdns. SS9: Lgh S ... 5J 31
Cliff Lift, The ... 6E 32
Clifford Cl. SS15: Lain ... 7F 15
Cliff Pde. SS9: Lgh S ... 5G 31
Cliff Rd. SS9: Lgh S ... 5J 31
Cliffsea Gro. SS9: Lgh S ... 4H 31
Cliffs Pavilion
Southend-on-Sea ... 6C 32
CLIFFTOWN ... 6D 32
Clifftown Pde. SS1: Sth S ... 6D 32
Clifftown Rd. SS1: Sth S ... 6E 32
Clifton Av. SS7: Ben ... 1B 28
Clifton Cl. SS7: Ben ... 1D 28
Clifton Dr. SS0: Wclf S ... 6B 32
Clifton M. SS1: Sth S ... 6E 32
Clifton Rd. SS4: Ashin ... 4J 13
SS8: Can I ... 5F 39
SS13: B Gif ... 5K 17
Clifton Ter. SS1: Sth S ... 6E 32
Clifton Wlk. SS7: Ben ... 1D 28
Clifton Way SS7: Ben ... 1C 28
Climmen Rd. SS8: Can I ... 3F 39
Clinton Rd. SS8: Can I ... 5B 38
Cloisters SS17: Stan H ... 5E 36
Cloisters, The SS15: Lain ... 6E 14
Clopton Grn. SS14: Bas ... 5K 15
Close, The SS5: Hock ... 2C 12
SS7: Ben ... 5D 28
SS7: Thun ... 4H 19
Clough Ho. SS0: Wclf S ... 1A 32
Clova Rd. SS9: Lgh S ... 3H 31
Clovelly Gdns. SS11: Wick ... 3E 8
Clover Cl. SS16: Vange ... 2C 26
Cloverleaf SS8: Can I ... 4K 39
Clover Way SS16: Vange ... 2C 26
Cluny Sq. SS2: Sth S ... 2G 33
Clusters, The SS2: Sth S ... 4D 32
Clyde Cres. SS6: Ray ... 3J 19
Clyst Ct. SS9: Lgh S ... 6F 21
Coachman Ct. SS4: R'fd ... 2C 22
Coach M. CM11: Bill ... 2H 5
Coahill Path SS14: Bas ... 3D 16
Coaster Steps *SS1: Sth S ... 6G 33*
(off Kursaal Way)
Cobbins, The CM0: Bur C ... 3C 40
Cobbins Chase CM0: Bur C ... 2C 40
Cobbins Cl. CM0: Bur C ... 2C 40
Cobbins Gro. CM0: Bur C ... 2C 40
Cobden Wlk. SS13: Pit ... 5G 17
(not continuous)
Cobham Rd. SS0: Wclf S ... 6A 32
Coburg La. SS16: Lan H ... 1B 24
Coburg Pl. CM3: Sth F ... 3H 7
Cockerell Cl. SS13: Bas ... 3F 17
Cockethurst Cl. SS0: Wclf S ... 1J 31
Codenham Grn. SS16: Bas ... 1K 25
Codenham Straight
SS16: Bas ... 1K 25
Cokefield Av. SS2: Sth S ... 2G 33
Coker Rd. SS8: Can I ... 6B 38
Colbert Av. SS1: Sth S ... 6J 33
Colbourne Cl. SS17: Stan H ... 4F 37
Colchester Cl. SS2: Sth S ... 3D 32
Colchester Rd. SS2: Sth S ... 3D 32
Coleman's Av. SS0: Wclf S ... 1B 32
Coleman St. SS2: Sth S ... 4E 32
College La. SS15: Lain ... 4D 14
College Way SS1: Sth S ... 5E 32
Collier Way SS1: Sth S ... 6G 33
Collindale Cl. SS8: Can I ... 4H 39
Collingwood SS7: Ben ... 1E 28
Collingwood Rd. CM3: Sth F ... 4K 7
SS16: Vange ... 1B 26
Collingwood Ter.
SS16: Vange ... 1B 26
Collingwood Wlk.
SS16: Vange ... 7B 16
Collingwood Way SS3: Shoe ... 3E 34
Collins Cl. SS17: Stan H ... 5E 36
Collins Ho. SS17: Corr ... 3F 37
Collins Way SS9: Lgh S ... 6J 21
Colman Cl. SS17: Stan H ... 4D 36
Colne Cl. CM3: Sth F ... 3J 7
Colne Dr. SS3: Shoe ... 3E 34
Colne Pl. SS16: Bas ... 1A 26
Coltishall Cl. SS11: Wick ... 5K 9
Colville Cl. SS17: Corr ... 2F 37
Colville M. CM12: Bill ... 2D 4
Colworth Cl. SS7: Hadl'gh ... 1K 29
Combined Court
Basildon ... 6J 15
Comet Way SS2: Sth S ... 6K 21
Comet Way Ind. Est.
SS2: Sth S ... 6K 21
Commercial Rd. SS0: Wclf S ... 1B 32
Commercial Way SS15: Lain ... 5A 14
Commodore Ho. SS14: Bas ... 6C 16
Common, The SS7: Thun ... 5G 19
Common App. SS7: Thun ... 6G 19
Commonhall La.
SS7: Hadl'gh ... 2K 29
Common La. SS7: Thun ... 5G 19
Common Rd. SS3: Gt W ... 1H 35
Compass Gdns. CM0: Bur C ... 4B 40
Compton Ct. SS8: Can I ... 6H 39
SS11: Wick ... 4G 9
Compton Ter. SS11: Wick ... 4G 9
Compton Wlk. SS15: Lain ... 5D 14
Concord Rangers FC ... 7D 38
Concord Rd. SS8: Can I ... 3D 38
Conifers SS7: Hadl'gh ... 2A 30
Coniston SS2: Sth S ... 5J 21
Coniston Cl. SS6: Ray ... 2A 20
Coniston Rd. SS7: Thun ... 5E 18
SS8: Can I ... 5E 38
Connaught Dr. CM3: Sth F ... 3G 7
Connaught Gdns. SS3: Shoe ... 6C 34
Connaught Rd. SS6: Ray ... 4C 20
Connaught Wlk. SS6: Ray ... 4C 20
Connaught Way CM12: Bill ... 2E 4
Conrad Ct. SS17: Stan H ... 6C 36
Conrad Rd. SS17: Stan H ... 5E 36
Constable Way SS3: Shoe ... 4F 35
Constitution Hill SS7: Ben ... 2D 28
Convent Cl. SS15: Lain ... 6E 14
Convent Rd. SS8: Can I ... 5F 39
Con Way SS7: Ben ... 2D 28
Conway Av. SS3: Gt W ... 1G 35
Cookham Ct. SS3: Shoe ... 2E 34
Cooks Grn. SS13: Bas ... 3G 17
Coombe Dr. SS16: Bas ... 4E 24
Coombe Ri. SS17: Stan H ... 5E 36
Coombe Rd. CM0: S'min ... 5G 41
Coombes Cl. CM12: Bill ... 3D 4
Coombes Cnr. SS9: Lgh S ... 1G 31
Coombes Gro. SS4: R'fd ... 2E 22
Coombewood Dr. SS7: Thun ... 7E 18
Coopersales SS15: Lain ... 6C 14
Coopers Dr. CM11: Bill ... 7A 4
Coopers Way SS2: Sth S ... 7E 22
Copdoek SS14: Bas ... 5A 16
Copelands SS4: Ashin ... 5K 13
Copford Av. SS6: Ray ... 3B 20
Copford Cl. CM11: Bill ... 5G 5
Copford Rd. CM11: Bill ... 5G 5
Copland Rd. SS17: Stan H ... 6D 36
Coppens Grn. SS12: Wick ... 5G 9
Copper Beeches SS7: Thun ... 5H 19
Copperfield CM11: Bill ... 7B 4
Copperfields SS15: Lain ... 5E 14
Coppice La. SS15: Bas ... 3H 15
Copse, The CM12: Bill ... 3E 4
Coptfold Cl. SS1: Sth S ... 4K 33
Coral Cl. CM3: Sth F ... 2G 7
Corasway SS7: Thun ... 7J 19
Cordelia Cres. SS6: Ray ... 1J 19
Cordwainers, The SS2: Sth S ... 7E 22
Corfe Cl. SS13: Pit ... 6F 17
Cormorant Cl. SS14: Bas ... 4A 16
Cornec Av. SS9: Lgh S ... 6D 20
Cornec Chase SS9: Lgh S ... 6E 20
Cornfields CM3: Sth F ... 2G 7
Cornflower Gdns. CM12: Bill ... 3D 4
Cornhill SS8: Can I ... 4J 39
Cornhill Av. SS5: Hock ... 4E 12
Cornish Gro. CM3: Sth F ... 4J 7
Cornwall Gdns. SS4: Ashin ... 6J 13
Cornwallis Dr. CM3: Sth F ... 3K 7
Cornwall Rd. SS13: B Gif ... 5K 17
Cornwell Cres. SS17: Stan H ... 4E 36
Cornworthy SS3: Shoe ... 4C 34
Corona Rd. SS8: Can I ... 3H 39
SS16: Lan H ... 2D 24
Coronation Cl. SS3: Gt W ... 1F 35
Coronation Rd. CM0: Bur C ... 6C 40
CORRINGHAM ... 3F 37
Corringham Rd. SS17: Stan H ... 6D 36
(Central Rd.)
SS17: Stan H ... 4G 37
(Warburtons)
Corsel Rd. SS8: Can I ... 5J 39
Corton Trad. Est. SS7: Thun ... 5D 18
Cosgrove Av. SS9: Lgh S ... 2D 30
Cossington Ct. SS0: Wclf S ... 5C 32
Cossington Rd. SS0: Wclf S ... 5C 32
Cotelands SS16: Vange ... 2D 26
Cotswold Av. SS6: Ray ... 1K 19
Cotswold Rd. SS0: Wclf S ... 5B 32
Cottages, The SS3: Shoe ... 5F 35
Cottesmore Cl. SS8: Can I ... 6F 39
Cottesmore Ct. SS9: Lgh S ... 3C 30
Cottesmore Gdns. SS9: Lgh S ... 4C 30
Cottis Cl. SS16: Lan H ... 2C 24
Coulter M. CM11: Bill ... 4F 5
County Court
Southend-on-Sea ... 5E 32
Courtauld Cl. SS13: Bas ... 2G 17
Courtauld Rd. SS13: Bas ... 3E 16
Courtlands CM12: Bill ... 5C 4
SS9: Lgh S ... 5D 20
Courtney Pk. Rd.
SS16: Lan H ... 7D 14
Courts, The SS6: Ray ... 1A 20
Courtyard, The CM0: S'min ... 5F 41
CM11: Bill ... 6G 5
Coventry Cl. SS5: Hull ... 2K 11
Coventry Hill SS5: Hull ... 2J 11
Cowslip Mead SS14: Bas ... 6K 15
Coxbridge Ct. CM12: Bill ... 5E 4
Coxes Cl. SS17: Stan H ... 4D 36
Coxes Farm Rd. CM11: Bill ... 6J 5
Coxs Cl. CM3: Sth F ... 2J 7
Craftsmans Sq. SS2: Sth S ... 7E 22
Cranbrook Av. SS7: Thun ... 1J 29
CRANES ... 2D 16
Cranes Cl. SS14: Bas ... 2D 16
Cranes Ct. SS14: Bas ... 4A 16
Cranes Farm Rd. SS14: Bas ... 4H 15
Cranes La. SS14: Bas ... 4A 16
Cranfield Ct. SS12: Wick ... 3E 8
Cranfield Pk. Av. SS12: Nth B ... 2K 17
Cranfield Pk. Ct. SS12: Wick ... 6F 9
Cranfield Pk. Rd. SS12: Wick ... 7F 9
Cranleigh Dr. SS9: Lgh S ... 3G 31
Cranleigh Gdns. SS5: Hull ... 2H 11
Cranley Av. SS0: Wclf S ... 4B 32
Cranley Gdns. SS3: Shoe ... 6C 34
Cranley Rd. SS0: Wclf S ... 5B 32
Cranmer Cl. CM12: Bill ... 1F 5
Cranston Av. SS0: Wclf S ... 7B 22
Craven Av. SS8: Can I ... 5E 38
Craven Cl. SS4: Ashin ... 6K 13
Crawford Chase SS12: Wick ... 6G 9
Crawford Cl. CM12: Bill ... 2G 5
Crawley Cl. SS17: Corr ... 2G 37
Craylands SS14: Bas ... 5D 16
(not continuous)
CRAYS HILL ... 6A 8
Crays Hill Rd. CM11: C Hill ... 6A 8
Crays Vw. CM12: Bill ... 7F 5
Creasy Ct. SS14: Bas ... 6D 16
Creek Rd. SS8: Can I ... 4H 39
CREEKSEA ... 5A 40
Creeksea La. CM0: Bur C ... 4A 40
Creeksea Pl. Cvn. Pk.
CM0: Bur C ... 5A 40
Creek Vw. SS16: Vange ... 2C 26
Creek Vw. Av. SS5: Hull ... 7G 7
Creekview Rd. CM3: Sth F ... 3K 7
Crescent, The SS7: Hadl'gh ... 2B 30
Crescent Cl. CM12: Bill ... 3D 4
Crescent Ct. SS9: Lgh S ... 4D 30
Crescent Gdns. CM12: Bill ... 3D 4
Crescent Pl. SS7: Hadl'gh ... 3B 30
Crescent Rd. CM12: Bill ... 3D 4
SS7: Ben ... 3D 28
SS8: Can I ... 5H 39
SS9: Lgh S ... 4D 30
Cressells SS15: Lain ... 6H 15
Crest, The SS9: Lgh S ... 6F 21
Crest Av. SS13: Pit ... 6G 17
Creswick Av. SS6: Ray ... 1J 19
Creswick Ct. SS6: Ray ... 1J 19
Cricketers Path *SS13: Bas ... 2E 16*
(off Cricketers Way)
Cricketers Retail Pk.
SS13: Bas ... 1F 17
Cricketers Way SS13: Bas ... 2E 16
Cricketfield Gro. SS9: Lgh S ... 3H 31
Crickhollow CM3: Sth F ... 5G 7
Cringle Lock CM3: Sth F ... 5J 7
CRIPPLEGATE ... 4H 41
Cripplegate CM0: S'min ... 4H 41
Crispins SS1: Sth S ... 4A 34
Croft, The SS6: Ray ... 4B 20
Croft Cl. SS7: Ben ... 7C 18
SS9: Lgh S ... 1G 31
Crofton Av. SS17: Corr ... 3F 37
Croft Rd. SS7: Ben ... 7B 18
Cromer Av. SS15: Lain ... 4D 14
Cromer Cl. SS15: Lain ... 4D 14
Cromer Rd. SS1: Sth S ... 5F 33
Crompton Av. SS15: Lain ... 4F 15
Crompton Cl. SS14: Bas ... 4H 15
Cromwell Av. CM12: Bill ... 4E 4
Cromwell Rd. SS2: Sth S ... 2E 32
SS5: Hock ... 5E 12
Cropenburg Wlk. SS8: Can I ... 3F 39
Crosby Rd. SS0: Wclf S ... 5K 31
Cross Av. SS12: Wick ... 5E 8
Crosse Courts SS15: Lain ... 7E 14
Crossfell Rd. SS7: Thun ... 5F 19
Crossfield Rd. SS2: Sth S ... 3H 33
Cross Grn. SS16: Bas ... 7H 15
Cross Rd. SS7: Thun ... 2H 29
SS13: B Gif ... 5K 17
(not continuous)
Crossway SS17: Stan H ... 4F 37
Crossway, The CM11: Bill ... 4H 5
(not continuous)
SS12: Wick ... 1J 17
Crossways SS8: Can I ... 4C 38
Crossways, The SS0: Wclf S ... 5J 31
Crouch Av. SS5: Hull ... 2J 11
Crouch Beck CM3: Sth F ... 3H 7
Crouch Dr. SS11: Wick ... 3F 9
Crouchmans Av. SS3: Gt W ... 1G 35
Crouchmans Ho. SS3: Shoe ... 3F 35
Crouch Mdw. SS5: Hull ... 6J 7
Crouch Pk. SS5: Hull ... 6J 7
Crouch Rd. CM0: Bur C ... 5D 40
Crouch St. SS15: Bas ... 3G 15
Crouchview Cl. SS11: Wick ... 4K 9
Crouch Vw. Cotts. CM3: Ret ... 5A 6
Crouch Vw. Cres. SS5: Hock ... 3G 13
Crouch Vw. Gro. SS5: Hull ... 7H 7
Crouch Way SS3: Shoe ... 5D 34
Crowborough Rd. SS2: Sth S ... 3D 32
Crown Av. SS13: Pit ... 6G 17
Crown Cl. SS13: Pit ... 6G 17
Crown Court
Southend-on-Sea ... 4D 32
Crown Gdns. SS6: Ray ... 2J 19
Crown Hgts. SS6: Ray ... 2K 19
Crown Hill SS6: Ray ... 2J 19
Crown Rd. CM11: Bill ... 5F 5
SS5: Hock ... 6B 12
Crown Way CM0: S'min ... 5F 41
Crown Yd. CM12: Bill ... 6E 4
Crowsnest, The CM0: Bur C ... 7D 40
Crowstone Av. SS0: Wclf S ... 6A 32
Crowstone Cl. SS0: Wclf S ... 4B 32
Crowstone Ct. *SS0: Wclf S ... 6B 32*
(off Holland Rd.)
Crowstone Rd. SS0: Wclf S ... 5A 32
Croxon Way CM0: Bur C ... 3C 40
Crystal Steps *SS1: Sth S ... 6G 33*
(off Beresford Rd.)
Cuckoo Cnr. SS2: Sth S ... 1C 32
Culverdown SS14: Bas ... 6J 15
Culver Ri. CM3: Sth F ... 3J 7
Cumberland Av. SS2: Sth S ... 3G 33
SS7: Ben ... 2C 28
Cumberland Dr. SS15: Lain ... 6C 14
Cumbrae M. SS12: Wick ... 6H 9
Cumming Rd. CM11: D'ham ... 1C 8
Cunningham Cl. SS3: Shoe ... 3F 35

A-Z Southend-on-Sea 47

Cunnignham Dr.—Eliot M.

Cunningham Dr. SS12: Wick 6G 9
Cupids Chase SS3: Shoe 2J 35
(not continuous)
Curlew Cres. SS16: Vange 2K 25
Curlew Dr. SS7: Ben 3C 28
Curling Tye SS14: Bas 5B 16
Curling Wlk. SS14: Bas 5B 16
Curtis Way SS6: Ray 7J 11
Cutlers Rd. CM3: Sth F 2J 7
Cygnet Ct. SS11: Wick 3F 9
Cypress Cl. SS15: Lain 3E 14
Czarina Ri. SS15: Lain 4G 15

D

Daarle Av. SS8: Can I 4E 38
Daines Cl. SS1: Sth S 4B 34
Daines Rd. CM11: Bill 5G 5
Daines Way SS1: Sth S 3A 34
Dale, The SS7: Thun 1G 29
Dalen Av. SS8: Can I 5E 38
Dale Rd. SS9: Lgh S 4D 30
Dales, The SS4: R'fd 1B 22
Dalmatia Rd. SS1: Sth S 4H 33
Dalmeny SS16: Lan H 1D 24
Daltons Fen SS13: Pit 4G 17
Dalwood SS3: Shoe 3D 34
Dalwood Gdns. SS7: Hadl'gh 1A 30
Dalys Rd. SS4: R'fd 2C 22
Danacre SS15: Lain 5D 14
Danbury Cl. SS9: Lgh S 1H 31
Danbury Down SS14: Bas 4B 16
Danbury Rd. SS6: Ray 1H 19
Dandies Chase SS9: Lgh S 5G 21
Dandies Cl. SS9: Lgh S 5F 21
Dandies Dr. SS9: Lgh S 5F 21
Danes Av. SS3: Shoe 6F 35
Danescroft Cl. SS9: Lgh S 1G 31
Danescroft Dr. SS9: Lgh S 1F 31
Danesfield SS7: Ben 3B 28
Danesleigh Gdns. SS9: Lgh S . . .1F 31
Dane St. SS3: Shoe 6G 35
D'Arcy Cl. CM0: Bur C 4D 40
Darell Way CM11: Bill 6H 5
(not continuous)
Darenth Rd. SS9: Lgh S 4D 30
Dark La. SS7: Thun 6G 19
Darlinghurst Gro. SS9: Lgh S . . .3J 31
Dartmouth Cl. SS6: Ray 6H 11
Darwin Ct. *SS14: Bas 5C 16*
(off Nightingale Gro.)
Datchet Dr. SS3: Shoe 2E 34
Davenants SS13: Bas 4F 17
David Av. SS11: Runw 1F 9
David Lloyd Leisure
Basildon 3K 15
Southend-on-Sea 6J 21
Davidson Gdns. SS12: Wick 6G 9
David's Wlk. CM11: Bill 5G 5
Dawberry Pl. CM3: Sth F 5H 7
Dawlish Cres. SS6: Ray 6H 11
Dawlish Dr. SS9: Lgh S 4G 31
Dawnings, The CM3: Sth F 2G 7
DAWS HEATH 6A 20
Daws Heath Rd. SS6: Ray 3K 19
SS7: Hadl'gh, Thun 6J 19
Dawson M. CM11: Bill 4F 5
Deacon Dr. SS15: Lain 5E 14
Debden Grn. SS16: Lan H 1E 24
Debden Way CM0: Bur C 4B 40
De Beauvoir Chase
CM11: D'ham, Ram H 1A 8
Dedham Cl. CM11: Bill 5G 5
Dedham Rd. CM11: Bill 5G 5
Deepdale SS7: Thun 7F 19
Deepdene SS16: Bas 7K 15
Deepdene Av. SS6: Ray 6G 11
(not continuous)
Deeping SS1: Sth S 5E 32
Deepwater Rd. SS8: Can I 5C 38
Deerbank Rd. CM11: Bill 4G 5
Deerhurst SS7: Thun 5H 19
Deerhurst Cl. SS7: Thun 5H 19
Deeside Wlk. SS12: Wick 6G 9
Deirdre Av. SS12: Wick 5D 8
Deirdre Cl. SS12: Wick 4D 8
Delaware Cres. SS3: Shoe 5D 34
Delaware Ho. SS3: Shoe 4C 34
Delaware Rd. SS3: Shoe 5C 34
Delder Av. SS8: Can I 6H 39
Delft Rd. SS8: Can I 4E 38
Delfzul Rd. SS8: Can I 4E 38
Delgada Rd. SS8: Can I 5H 39
Delhi Rd. SS13: Pit 6G 17
Delimands SS15: Lain 6H 15
Delius Way SS17: Stan H 4C 36
Dell, The SS11: Wick 4G 9
SS16: Vange 2K 25
Delmar Gdns. SS11: Wick 1E 8
Delmores SS16: Lan H 2E 24
Delview SS8: Can I 3D 38
Delvins SS13: Bas 4E 16
Denbigh Rd. SS15: Lain 7D 14
Dencourt Cres. SS14: Bas 7D 16
Dene Cl. SS6: Ray 7H 11
Dene Gdns. SS6: Ray 7H 11
Denehurst Gdns. SS16: Lan H . . .1A 24
Denesmere SS7: Ben 1C 28
Deneway SS16: Vange 3B 26
Dengayne SS14: Bas 6B 16
Dengie 100 Sports Cen. 6C 40
Denham Rd. SS8: Can I 4E 38
Denham Va. SS6: Ray 2G 19
Dennington Cres. SS14: Bas 5B 16
Denton App. SS0: Wclf S 7A 22
Denton Av. SS0: Wclf S 7A 22
Denton Cl. SS0: Wclf S 7A 22
Denver Dr. SS13: Bas 3G 17
Denys Dr. SS14: Bas 3D 16
Derby Cl. CM11: Bill 2H 5
SS16: Lan H 1B 24
Derbydale SS4: Ashin 5J 13
Derek Gdns. SS2: Sth S 7C 22
Dering Cres. SS9: Lgh S 5F 21
Derventer Av. SS8: Can I 2E 38
Derwent Av. SS6: Ray 2A 20
Dessons Ct. SS17: Corr 3F 37
Devereux Path SS13: Bas 3F 17
Devereux Rd. SS1: Sth S 6E 32
Devereux Way CM12: Bill 2E 4
Devon Gdns. SS4: Ashin 6J 13
Devonshire Cl. SS15: Lain 4C 14
Devonshire Rd. CM0: Bur C 5C 40
CM0: S'min 5F 41
SS15: Lain 4C 14
Devon Way SS8: Can I 3F 39
Dewlands SS14: Bas 5J 15
Dewsgreen SS16: Vange 1C 26
Dewyk Rd. SS8: Can I 3G 39
Diamond Cl. SS6: Ray 7E 10
Dickens Cl. SS2: Sth S 3F 33
Dickens Ct. SS15: Lain 5F 15
Dickens Dr. SS15: Lain 5E 14
Dickens M. SS12: Wick 6F 9
Digby Rd. SS17: Corr 2H 37
Dinant Av. SS8: Can I 3C 38
Disraeli Rd. SS6: Lgh S, Ray . . .3D 20
Ditton Ct. Rd. SS0: Wclf S 5B 32
Dixon Ct. SS13: Pit 6F 17
Dobsons Cl. SS6: Ray 3A 20
Dobsons Ho. SS6: Ray 3A 20
Doctors La. CM0: Bur C 6D 40
Doesgate La. RM14: Bulp 4A 24
Doeshill Dr. SS12: Wick 4G 9
Doggetts Cl. SS4: R'fd 1D 22
Dollant Av. SS8: Can I 5E 38
Dolphin Gdns. CM12: Bill 2D 4
Dolphins SS0: Wclf S 7B 22
Dome Village, The SS5: Hock . . .2C 12
Donald Thorn Cl. SS12: Wick 5F 9
Donside Wlk. SS12: Wick 6F 9
Dorchester Rd. CM12: Bill 2E 4
Dordells SS15: Lain 6G 15
Doric Av. SS4: Ashin 6K 13
Dorothy Farm Rd. SS6: Ray 3C 20
Dorothy Gdns. SS7: Thun 7F 19
Dorset Gdns. SS4: Ashin 6J 13
Dorset Rd. CM0: Bur C 6D 40
Dorset Way CM12: Bill 2E 4
SS8: Can I 3E 38
(off Hilton Rd.)
Doublegate La. SS11: Raw 6K 9
Doublet M. CM11: Bill 2H 5
Douglas Dr. SS12: Wick 6F 9
Douglas Rd. SS7: Hadl'gh 2B 30
Doulton Way SS4: Ashin 5J 13
Dovecote SS3: Shoe 3E 34
Dovedale SS8: Can I 3H 39
Dovedale Cl. SS16: Lan H 1C 24
Dove Dr. SS7: Ben 3B 28
Dovercliff Rd. SS8: Can I 5J 39
Dovervelt Rd. SS8: Can I 3F 39
Dover Way SS13: Pit 7F 17
Dovesgate SS7: Ben 1B 28
Doves M. SS15: Lain 3F 15
Dow Ct. CM0: S'min 5F 41
Dowland Cl. SS17: Stan H 4C 36
Dowland Wlk. SS15: Lain 5E 14
Downer Rd. SS7: Ben 1D 28
Downer Rd. Nth. SS7: Thun 7E 18
Downesway SS7: Ben 2D 28
Downey Cl. SS14: Bas 5A 16
Down Hall Cl. SS6: Ray 7H 11
Downhall Pk. Way SS6: Ray 5G 11
Down Hall Rd. SS6: Ray 1J 19
Downham Rd. SS8: Can I 5E 38
SS11: Runw 1E 8
Downleaze CM3: Sth F 2J 7
Downs Gro. SS16: Vange 2B 26
Dragon Cl. CM0: Bur C 5B 40
Drake Cl. SS7: Thun 1J 29
Drake Ct. SS14: Bas 7D 16
Drake Rd. SS0: Wclf S 5A 32
SS15: Lain 6F 15
Drakes, The SS3: Shoe 4E 34
Drakes Way SS6: Ray 7J 11
Drapers Rd. CM3: Sth F 2J 7
Drewsteignton SS3: Shoe 4D 34
Driftway SS16: Vange 2D 26
Drive, The CM3: Sth F 4F 7
(Celeborn St.)
CM3: Sth F 2F 7
(Ferrers Rd.)
SS0: Wclf S 4K 31
SS4: R'fd 2D 22
SS5: Hull 7H 7
SS6: Ray 4D 20
Driveway, The SS8: Can I 6F 39
Droitwich Av. SS2: Sth S 4H 33
Drummond Pl. SS12: Wick 6G 9
Dryden Av. SS2: Sth S 3F 33
DRY STREET 4G 25
Dry St.
SS16: Bas, Lan H, Vange . . .3E 24
Drywoods CM3: Sth F 5H 7
Dubarry Cl. SS7: Thun 7F 19
Duke Pl. SS15: Lain 4G 15
Dukes Av. CM0: S'min 6G 41
Dukes Farm Cl. CM12: Bill 2G 5
Dukes Farm Rd. CM12: Bill 3F 5
Dukes Rd. CM11: Bill 3G 5
Dulverton Av. SS0: Wclf S 1J 31
Dulverton Cl. SS0: Wclf S 7J 21
Dulwich Av. SS15: Lain 4E 14
Dunbar Pl. SS12: Wick 6G 9
Duncan Cl. SS12: Wick 6H 9
Dundee Av. SS9: Lgh S 3D 30
Dundee Cl. SS9: Lgh S 3E 30
Dundee Ct. SS14: Bas 4D 16
Dundonald Dr. SS9: Lgh S 4H 31
Dunfane CM11: Bill 2G 5
Dungannon Chase SS1: Sth S . . .6B 34
Dungannon Dr. SS1: Sth S 6B 34
Dunkirk Rd. CM0: Bur C 6D 40
Dunlin Cl. CM3: Sth F 1H 7
Dunlin Dr. SS14: Bas 4A 16
Dunstable Rd. SS17: Stan H 4C 36
Dunster Av. SS0: Wclf S 7J 21
Dunton Ford Link SS15: Lain 4A 14
Dunton Pk. Cvn. Site
CM13: Dun 6A 14
Dunton Rd. CM12: L Bur 3A 14
SS15: Lain 3A 14
Dunton Vw. CM13: Dun 7A 14
Durants Wlk. SS12: Wick 5F 9
Durban La. SS15: Bas 2H 15
Durdans, The SS16: Lan H 1D 24
Durham Rd. SS2: Sth S 3H 33
SS4: Ashin 6H 13
SS15: Lain 6B 14
Durham Way SS6: Ray 6H 11
Durley Av. SS12: Wick 3B 8
Durley Cl. SS7: Ben 1E 28
Durrington Cl. SS16: Bas 7A 16
Dutch Cottage
Rayleigh 2J 19
Dutch Cottage Mus.
Canvey Island 4A 38
DUTCH VILLAGE 4B 38
Duxford SS11: Wick 5J 9
Dyke Cres. SS8: Can I 4B 38
Dynevor Gdns. SS9: Lgh S 4D 30

E

Eagle Way SS3: Shoe 3E 34
Earleswood SS7: Ben 1D 28
Earl Mountbatten Dr.
CM12: Bill 3D 4
Earls Hall Av. SS2: Sth S 2B 32
Earls Hall Pde. SS2: Sth S 1C 32
East Beach Cvn. Pk.
SS3: Shoe 5G 35
Eastbourne Gro. SS0: Wclf S 2A 32
East Bri. Rd. CM3: Sth F 2H 7
Eastbrooks SS13: Pit 5F 17
Eastbrooks M. SS13: Pit 5F 17
Eastbrooks Pl. SS13: Pit 5F 17
Eastbury Av. SS4: R'fd 7K 13
Eastcheap SS6: Ray 7G 11
Eastcote Gro. SS2: Sth S 2H 33
East Cres. SS8: Can I 4D 38
Eastern Av. SS2: Sth S 2D 32
SS7: Ben 7C 18
Eastern Cl. SS2: Sth S 2E 32
Eastern Esplanade SS1: Sth S . . .6G 33
SS8: Can I 7G 39
Eastern Rd. CM0: Bur C 4D 40
SS6: Ray 4H 19
Eastfield Rd. SS8: Can I 3H 39
SS15: Bas 2H 15
Eastgate SS14: Bas 6K 15
Eastgate Bus. Cen. *SS14: Bas . . .6K 15*
(off Southernhay)
Eastgate Shop. Cen.
SS14: Bas 6K 15
E. Hanningfield Rd. CM3: Ret 1A 6
Eastleigh Rd. SS7: Ben 4E 28
Eastley SS16: Bas 1J 25
East Mayne SS13: Bas 5D 16
Easton End SS15: Lain 6C 14
East Sq. SS14: Bas 6K 15
East St. SS2: Sth S 3D 32
SS4: R'fd 2D 22
SS9: Lgh S 5G 31
East Thorpe SS14: Bas 6A 16
East Thurrock United FC 4H 37
Eastview Dr. SS6: Ray 6H 11
East Wlk. SS14: Bas 6K 15
Eastways SS8: Can I 3D 38
EASTWOOD 6G 21
Eastwood Blvd. SS0: Wclf S 2J 31
EASTWOODBURY 6A 22
Eastwoodbury Cl. SS2: Sth S 6B 22
Eastwoodbury Cres.
SS2: Sth S 6C 22
Eastwoodbury La. SS2: Sth S . . .6K 21
(not continuous)
Eastwood Ind. Est.
SS9: Lgh S 6E 20
Eastwood La. Sth.
SS0: Wclf S 3K 31
Eastwood Old Rd. SS9: Lgh S . . .5B 20
Eastwood Pk. Cl. SS9: Lgh S . . .6G 21
Eastwood Pk. Dr. SS9: Lgh S . . .5G 21
Eastwood Ri. SS9: Lgh S 5D 20
Eastwood Rd. SS6: Ray 2K 19
SS9: Lgh S 2F 31
Eastwood Rd. Nth.
SS9: Lgh S 1E 30
Eaton Cl. CM12: Bill 2E 4
Eaton Ct. SS14: Bas 6J 15
Eaton Rd. SS9: Lgh S 3E 30
Eccleston Gdns. CM12: Bill 2E 4
Edgecotts SS16: Bas 1G 25
Edinburgh Av. SS9: Lgh S 3D 30
SS17: Corr 3F 37
Edinburgh Cl. SS6: Ray 6F 11
Edinburgh Way SS13: Pit 6F 17
Edith Cl. SS8: Can I 5C 38
Edith Rd. SS2: Sth S 3D 32
SS8: Can I 5B 38
Edith Way SS17: Corr 2G 37
Edward Cl. CM12: Bill 2D 4
SS4: Ashin 5J 13
Edward Gdns. SS11: Wick 3F 9
Edwardian Club, The (Bowling Alley)
Billericay 4E 4
Edwin Hall Vw. CM3: Sth F 1G 7
Egbert Gdns. SS11: Runw 2F 9
Egerton Dr. SS16: Lan H 7A 14
(Burr Cl.)
SS16: Lan H 2C 24
(Mollys Dr.)
Egret Cl. SS14: Bas 4A 16
Eisenhower Rd. SS15: Lain 6C 14
Eldbert Cl. SS2: Sth S 3J 33
Eldeland SS15: Lain 5G 15
Elder Av. SS12: Wick 5D 8
Elderberry Cl. SS16: Lan H 7D 14
Elderstep Av. SS8: Can I 5J 39
Elderton Rd. SS0: Wclf S 5B 32
Elder Tree Rd. SS8: Can I 4G 39
Elder Way SS12: Wick 5E 8
Elderwick Path *SS8: Can I 4G 39*
(off Waalwyk Dr.)
Eldon Way SS5: Hock 5D 12
Eldon Way Ind. Est.
SS5: Hock 5E 12
Eleanor Chase SS12: Wick 4E 8
Electric Av. SS0: Wclf S 4A 32
Elgar Cl. SS7: Thun 6B 18
SS15: Lain 4F 15
Elham Dr. SS13: Pit 7G 17
Eliot Cl. SS12: Wick 6E 8
Eliot M. SS2: Sth S 3F 33

48 A-Z Southend-on-Sea

Elizabeth Av.—Four Sisters Way

Elizabeth Av. SS6: Ray 3J 19
Elizabeth Cl. SS5: Hawk 7E 12
Elizabeth Dr. SS12: Wick 3D 8
Elizabeth Ho. SS7: Hadl'gh 2J 29
SS9: Lgh S 6F 21
Elizabeth Rd. SS1: Sth S 7H 33
Elizabeth Twr. *SS2: Sth S 4D 32*
(off Baxter Av.)
Elizabeth Way SS7: Thun 1J 29
SS15: Lain 7E 14
Ellenbrook Cl. SS9: Lgh S 2G 31
Ellesmere Rd. SS4: Ashin 2J 13
SS8: Can I 5C 38
Ellie Cl. SS17: Stan H 5C 36
Elliot Cl. CM3: Sth F 4K 7
Ellswood SS15: Lain 3F 15
Elm Bank Pl. SS17: Horn H 3A 36
Elmbrook Cl. SS14: Bas 4A 16
Elm Cl. SS3: Shoe 5E 34
SS6: Ray 1K 19
Elm Dr. SS6: Ray 1K 19
Elmer App. SS1: Sth S 5E 32
Elmer Av. SS1: Sth S 5E 32
Elmer Sq. *SS1: Sth S 5E 32*
(off Elmer Av.)
Elm Grn. CM11: Bill 5J 5
SS13: Pit 7E 16
Elm Gro. SS1: Sth S 4A 34
SS5: Hull 1H 11
Elm Ho. *SS8: Can I 7F 39*
(off Western Esplanade)
Elmhurst Av. SS7: Ben 1B 28
Elm Rd. CM3: Sth F 2G 7
SS3: Shoe 5E 34
SS7: Hadl'gh 3K 29
SS8: Can I 5G 39
SS9: Lgh S 3G 31
(not continuous)
SS11: Wick 3F 9
SS13: B Gif 3J 17
Elms Bus. Pk. SS12: Wick 7G 9
Elms Ct. SS0: Wclf S 7H 21
Elmsleigh Dr. SS9: Lgh S 2G 31
Elmstead Cl. SS17: Corr 2H 37
Elmtree Rd. SS16: Vange 1D 26
Elm Vw. Rd. SS7: Ben 2B 28
Elmwood Av. SS5: Hawk 7E 12
Elounda Ct. SS7: Ben 1D 28
Elronds Rest CM3: Sth F 4G 7
Elsden Chase CM0: S'min 5G 41
Elsenham Ct. SS6: Ray 1H 19
Elsenham Cres. SS14: Bas 6D 16
Elsenham M. SS14: Bas 6D 16
Elsinor Av. SS8: Can I 2D 38
Elverston Cl. SS15: Lain 4F 15
Elverston Side SS15: Lain 4F 15
Ely Cl. CM0: S'min 5G 41
Ely Rd. SS2: Sth S 3F 33
Ely Way SS6: Ray 7G 11
SS14: Bas 5C 16
Emanuel Rd. SS16: Lan H 1D 24
Embankment, The SS5: Hock 2D 12
Ember Way CM0: Bur C 4B 40
Emily White Ct. SS11: Wick 3H 9
Empire Cinema
Basildon 3K 15
Endeavour Dr. SS14: Bas 3K 15
Endway SS7: Hadl'gh 3K 29
Enfield Rd. SS11: Raw 4A 10
Englefield Cl. SS5: Hawk 7G 13
Ennismore Gdns. SS2: Sth S 2E 32
Ensign Cl. SS9: Lgh S 4J 31
Enterprise Cen., The
SS14: Bas 2C 16
Enterprise Way SS11: Wick 5H 9
Epping Cl. SS9: Lgh S 5G 21
Epsom Cl. CM11: Bill 2H 5
Epsom M. CM0: S'min 5H 41
Eric Rd. SS13: B Gif 6K 17
Eros Av. SS2: Sth S 5J 33
Erskine Pl. SS12: Wick 5G 9
Esplanade, The SS5: Hull 7G 7
Esplanade Ct. SS1: Sth S 7H 33
Esplanade Gdns. SS0: Wclf S 5K 31
Essex Cl. SS6: Ray 3B 20
SS8: Can I 6E 38
SS15: Lain 6D 14
Essex Gdns. SS9: Lgh S 1G 31
Essex Rd. CM0: Bur C 5D 40
SS8: Can I 4G 39
Essex St. SS1: Sth S 5E 32
Essex Way SS7: Ben 4D 28
Essex Yacht Club 6G 31
Estate Rd. SS7: Hadl'gh 2B 30
Estuary Gdns. SS3: Gt W 2J 35
Estuary Lodge SS1: Sth S 7J 33
Estuary M. SS3: Shoe 6E 34
Ethelbert Rd. SS4: Ashin 2J 13
Etheldore Av. SS5: Hock 3E 12
Ethelred Gdns. SS11: Runw 2F 9
Ethel Rd. SS6: Ray 4D 20
Eton Cl. SS8: Can I 3F 39
Eton Ho. SS15: Lain 4D 14
Eton Wlk. SS3: Shoe 2E 34
Evelyn Rd. SS5: Hock 6E 12
Everard Rd. SS14: Bas 4E 16
Everest SS6: Ray 6H 11
Everest Ri. CM12: Bill 6D 4
Everglades, The SS7: Hadl'gh 3B 30
Evergreen SS8: Can I 4J 39
Evergreen Ct. SS12: Wick 5E 8
EVERSLEY 6H 17
Eversley Ct. SS7: Thun 5C 18
Eversley Leisure Cen. 6H 17
Eversley Rd. SS7: Thun 5B 18
SS13: Pit 7H 17
EVES CORNER 3C 40
Evolve Gym *5D 32*
(off London Rd.)
Ewan Cl. SS9: Lgh S 2C 30
Ewan Way SS9: Lgh S 2C 30
Exeter Cl. SS3: Shoe 3F 35
SS14: Bas 4D 16
Exeter Ho. SS3: Shoe 3F 35
Exford Av. SS0: Wclf S 7J 21
Exhibition La. SS3: Gt W 1F 35
Exmouth Dr. SS6: Ray 6H 11
Eynsham Way SS13: Bas 3E 16
Eyott Sailing Club 5F 7

F

Failand M. SS17: Stan H 3D 36
Fairburn Cl. SS1: Sth S 5G 33
Fairfax Av. SS13: Bas 4G 17
Fairfax Dr. SS0: Wclf S 3K 31
Fairfield SS3: Gt W 1G 35
Fairfield Cres. SS9: Lgh S 6H 21
Fairfield Gdns. SS9: Lgh S 6G 21
Fairfield Ri. CM12: Bill 7D 4
(not continuous)
Fairfield Rd. SS9: Lgh S 6G 21
FAIR HAVENS HOSPICE 5K 31
Fairhouse Ct. SS14: Bas 6B 16
Fairland Cl. SS6: Ray 6J 11
Fairlawn Gdns. SS2: Sth S 7C 22
Fairlawns SS1: Sth S 6K 33
Fairleigh Av. SS13: Pit 7H 17
Fairleigh Dr. SS9: Lgh S 4F 31
Fairleigh Rd. SS13: Pit 7H 17
Fairlight Rd. SS7: Hadl'gh 2J 29
Fairlop Av. SS8: Can I 4E 38
Fairlop Gdns. SS14: Bas 6B 16
Fairman Cl. CM0: S'min 5F 41
Fair Mead SS14: Bas 4A 16
Fairmead SS6: Ray 7F 11
Fairmead Av. SS0: Wclf S 4A 32
SS7: Hadl'gh 7A 20
Fairsted SS14: Bas 6J 15
Fairview CM12: Bill 6E 4
SS8: Can I 3D 38
Fairview Av. SS17: Stan H 6C 36
Fairview Chase
SS17: Stan H 7C 36
Fairview Cl. SS7: Thun 5C 18
Fairview Cres. SS7: Thun 5C 18
Fairview Dr. SS0: Wclf S 1A 32
Fairview Gdns. SS9: Lgh S 3E 30
(not continuous)
Fair Vw. Lodge SS9: Lgh S 3E 30
Fairview Rd. SS14: Bas 6B 16
(Pemberry Hall)
SS14: Bas 7C 16
(The Witterings)
Fairview Wlk. SS7: Thun 5C 18
Fairville M. SS0: Wclf S 3A 32
Fairway SS12: Wick 1J 17
Fairway, The SS7: Thun 5C 18
SS9: Lgh S 7E 20
SS16: Bas 3E 24
Fairway Dr. CM0: Bur C 5C 40
Fairway Gdns. SS9: Lgh S 7E 20
Fairway Gdns. Cl.
SS9: Lgh S 7E 20
Fairways SS1: Sth S 5K 33
Falbro Cres. SS7: Hadl'gh 1K 29
Falcon Cl. SS6: Ray 1H 19
SS9: Lgh S 7H 21
Falcon Pk. SS14: Bas 4H 15
Falcon Rd. CM0: S'min 5F 41
Falcon Way SS3: Shoe 3E 34
SS16: Bas 1A 26
Falkenham End SS14: Bas 5A 16
Falkenham Path SS14: Bas 5A 16
Falkenham Ri. SS14: Bas 5A 16
Falkenham Row SS14: Bas 5A 16
Falklands Rd. CM0: Bur C 5C 40
Fallowfield SS3: Shoe 3D 34
Fallows, The SS8: Can I 2D 38
Falstaff Pl. SS16: Lan H 7C 14
Falstones SS15: Lain 6F 15
Fambridge Dr. SS12: Wick 5G 9
Fambridge Rd. SS4: Ashin 2H 13
Fane Rd. SS7: Thun 4D 18
(not continuous)
Fanton Av. SS12: Wick 1K 17
Fanton Chase SS11: Wick 5J 9
Fanton Gdns. SS11: Wick 5K 9
Fanton Hall Cotts.
SS12: Nth B 2A 18
Fanton Wlk. SS11: Wick 4K 9
Faraday Ct. *SS16: Bas 7J 15*
(off Bessemer Cl.)
Faraday Rd. SS9: Lgh S 6E 20
Faraday Way SS14: Bas 5D 16
Farm Cres. SS11: Bat 6C 6
Farm Rd. SS8: Can I 3F 39
Farm Vw. SS6: Ray 6H 11
Farm Way SS7: Thun 6H 19
Farnaby Way SS17: Stan H 4C 36
Farne Dr. SS12: Wick 6H 9
Farnes Av. SS12: Wick 5E 8
Farnham Av. SS11: Wick 2E 8
Farriers Dr. CM12: Bill 2E 4
Farriers Way SS2: Sth S 7D 22
Farringdon Service Rd.
SS1: Sth S 5E 32
Fastnet SS2: Sth S 5J 21
Fauners SS16: Bas 7J 15
Faversham Lodge *SS1: Sth S 7J 33*
(off Eastern Esplanade)
Fawcett Dr. SS15: Lain 3G 15
Featherby Way SS4: R'fd 3E 22
Feeches Rd. SS2: Sth S 7A 22
Feering Dr. SS14: Bas 7D 16
Feering Grn. SS14: Bas 7D 16
Feering Rd. CM11: Bill 5G 5
Feering Row SS14: Bas 7D 16
Fellcroft SS13: Pit 6G 17
FELMORE 4F 17
Felmore Ct. SS13: Bas 4F 17
Felmores SS13: Bas 4E 16
Felmores End SS13: Bas 4F 17
Felstead Cl. SS7: Ben 1D 28
Felstead Rd. SS7: Ben 1D 28
Felsted Rd. CM11: Bill 5G 5
Fengates CM3: Sth F 2G 7
Fenn Cl. CM3: Sth F 2G 7
Fenners Way SS13: Bas 2E 16
Fennfields Rd. CM3: Sth F 2F 7
Fenton Way SS15: Lain 5B 14
Fenwick Way SS8: Can I 2E 38
Fermoy Rd. SS1: Sth S 5A 34
Fernbank CM12: Bill 6D 4
Fernbrook Av. SS1: Sth S 5H 33
Fern Cl. CM12: Bill 3F 5
Fern Ct. SS17: Stan H 4D 36
Ferndale Cl. SS15: Lain 6D 14
Ferndale Cres. SS8: Can I 6F 39
Ferndale Rd. SS2: Sth S 3G 33
SS6: Ray 5H 11
Ferndown Cl. SS2: Sth S 5G 33
SS17: Stan H 7B 36
Fern Hill SS16: Lan H 1E 24
Fernlea Pl. CM11: Bill 4G 5
Fernlea Rd. CM0: Bur C 5C 40
SS7: Ben 2E 28
Fernleigh Dr. SS9: Lgh S 4J 31
Fernside Cl. SS17: Corr 2H 37
Fern Wlk. SS8: Can I 5D 38
SS16: Lan H 1A 24
Fernwood SS7: Hadl'gh 1A 30
Ferrers Rd. CM3: Sth F 2F 7
Ferris Steps SS1: Sth S 6G 33
Ferrymead SS8: Can I 3D 38
Ferry Rd. CM0: Bur C 4A 40
SS5: Hull 7J 7
SS7: Ben 5D 28
Festival Bus. Pk. SS14: Bas 3K 15
Festival Leisure Pk.
SS14: Bas 3K 15
Festival Link SS14: Bas 4K 15
Festival Way SS14: Bas 3K 15
Fetherston Rd. SS17: Stan H 5D 36
Fielders, The SS8: Can I 6D 38
Fieldfare CM11: Bill 7G 5
Fielding Way SS0: Wclf S 3B 32
Field Vw. SS7: Ben 7C 18
Fieldway SS12: Wick 1H 17
SS13: Pit 1G 27
Fifth Av. SS7: Thun 6G 19
SS8: Can I 4C 38
SS11: Wick 5J 9
Fillebrook Av. SS9: Lgh S 3J 31
Finches, The SS7: Thun 5G 19
Finches Chase SS15: Lain 5G 15
Finches Cl. SS17: Corr 2J 37
Finchfield SS6: Ray 3K 19
Finchingfield Way SS12: Wick 6E 8
Finchland Vw. CM3: Sth F 4H 7
Finchley Rd. SS0: Wclf S 5B 32
Fir Ct. SS15: Lain 3E 14
Firfield Rd. SS7: Thun 6H 19
Firle, The SS16: Lan H 2E 24
Firmans SS16: Lan H 2D 24
Firs, The SS8: Can I 3D 38
First Av. CM12: Bill 7C 4
SS0: Wclf S 5K 31
SS5: Hull 2K 11
SS7: Thun 6G 19
SS8: Can I 4B 38
SS11: Wick 5J 9
SS16: Lan H 1A 24
SS17: Stan H 4D 36
Fir Tree Cl. SS5: Hawk 7G 13
Fir Wlk. SS8: Can I 3D 38
Fitness 4 Less
Southend-on-Sea *5E 32*
(within The Victoria Shop. Cen.)
Fitness First
Basildon 3K 15
Fitzroy Cl. CM12: Bill 3E 4
Fitzwarren SS3: Shoe 3D 34
Fitzwilliam Rd. SS7: Hadl'gh 3J 29
Five Oaks SS7: Thun 1H 29
Flamboro Cl. SS9: Lgh S 6F 21
Flamboro Wlk. SS9: Lgh S 6F 21
Fleethall Rd. SS4: R'fd 4E 22
Fleet Rd. SS7: Ben 3D 28
Fleetway SS16: Vange 1D 26
Fleetwood SS8: Can I 6J 39
Fleetwood Av. SS0: Wclf S 4A 32
Flemings Farm Rd.
SS9: Lgh S 4F 21
Flemming Av. SS9: Lgh S 2F 31
Flemming Cres. SS9: Lgh S 2F 31
Fletcher Ct. CM11: Bill 5H 5
Fletcher Dr. SS12: Wick 5G 9
Fletchers SS16: Bas 2G 25
Fletchers Sq. SS2: Sth S 7E 22
Flint Cl. SS16: Lan H 7B 14
Florence Cl. SS7: Hadl'gh 2K 29
Florence Ct. SS16: Lan H 7E 14
Florence Gdns. SS7: Hadl'gh 2J 29
Florence Neale Ho.
SS8: Can I 5E 38
(off Kitkatts Rd.)
Florence Rd. SS8: Can I 4G 39
Florence Way SS16: Lan H 7D 14
FOBBING 2K 37
Fobbing Farm Cl. SS16: Bas 2J 25
Fobbing Rd. SS17: Corr 3H 37
Fodderwick SS14: Bas 7J 15
Foksville Rd. SS8: Can I 5G 39
Fold, The SS14: Bas 6K 15
Folly Chase SS5: Hock 5B 12
Folly La. SS5: Hock 5B 12
Font Cl. SS15: Lain 6E 14
Fonteyn Cl. SS15: Lain 4E 14
Ford Cl. SS15: Lain 6C 14
Ford Ho. SS3: Shoe 6F 35
Forest Av. SS1: Sth S 6F 33
Forester Ct. CM12: Bill 4D 4
Forest Glade SS16: Lan H 1A 24
Forest Glade Ct. SS7: Ben 7B 18
Fore St. SS15: Bas 2G 15
Forest Vw. Dr. SS9: Lgh S 2C 30
Forfar Cl. SS9: Lgh S 3D 30
Forge, The SS12: Wick 4F 9
Forge Way SS1: Sth S 7G 33
Forrest Cl. CM3: Sth F 3G 7
Fortescue Chase SS1: Sth S 4K 33
Fortune Steps *SS1: Sth S 6G 33*
(off Kursaal Way)
Fort William Rd. SS16: Vange 3K 25
Forum, The 5E 32
Forum, The SS2: Sth S 7E 22
Fossetts Dr. SS2: Sth S 1G 33
Fossetts Way SS2: Sth S 7F 23
Fostal Cl. SS9: Lgh S 2G 31
Foster Rd. SS8: Can I 4G 39
Foulgar Cl. CM3: Sth F 2J 7
Foundry Bus. Pk. SS5: Hock 5E 12
Foundry La. CM0: Bur C 5B 40
Fountain La. SS5: Hock 6B 12
Four Sisters Cl. SS9: Lgh S 7H 21
Four Sisters Way SS9: Lgh S 6H 21

A-Z Southend-on-Sea 49

Griffin Av. SS8: Can I — 3G 39
Grimston Rd. SS14: Bas — 4D 16
Grosvenor Ct. SS0: Wclf S — 6A 32
  SS2: Sth S — 3D 32
Grosvenor Gdns. CM12: Bill — 3E 4
Grosvenor Mans. SS0: Wclf S — 5A 32
  (off Grosvenor Rd.)
Grosvenor M. SS0: Wclf S — 6A 32
Grosvenor Rd. SS0: Wclf S — 6A 32
  SS6: Ray — 6E 10
  SS7: Ben — 5E 28
Grove, The CM11: Bill — 2G 5
  SS3: Sth S — 3F 33
  SS17: Stan H — 7D 36
Grove Av. SS16: Lan H — 2D 24
Grove Cl. SS6: Ray — 2B 20
Grove Ct. SS0: Wclf S — 2A 31
  SS6: Ray — 3C 20
Grove Hill SS9: Lgh S — 5D 20
Grovelands SS2: Sth S — 3H 33
Grovelands Rd. SS12: Wick — 5F 9
Grove Lodge SS3: Shoe — 5G 35
  (off Gunners Rd.)
Grove Rd. CM12: Bill — 5D 4
  SS6: Lgh S, Ray — 4B 20
  SS7: Ben — 3D 28
  SS8: Can I — 4G 39
  SS17: Stan H — 7D 36
Grover St. SS1: Sth S — 5E 32
Grover Wlk. SS17: Corr — 4F 37
Grove Wlk. SS3: Shoe — 5E 34
Grovewood Av. SS9: Lgh S — 5D 20
Grovewood Cl. SS9: Lgh S — 5D 20
Guernsey Gdns. SS11: Wick — 2F 9
Guildford Ct. SS2: Sth S — 4E 32
  (off Guildford Rd.)
Guildford Rd. SS2: Sth S — 4E 32
Guild Way CM3: Sth F — 3J 7
Gunfleet SS3: Shoe — 5C 34
Gun Hill Pl. SS16: Bas — 7A 16
Gunn Cl. SS6: Ray — 7E 10
Gunners Ho. SS3: Shoe — 7E 34
Gunners Ri. SS3: Shoe — 7E 34
Gunners Rd. SS3: Shoe — 5G 35
Gusted Hall La. SS5: Hawk — 2G 21
Guys Farm Rd. CM3: Sth F — 3H 7
Gwendalen Av. SS8: Can I — 4H 39

H

Haarlem Rd. SS8: Can I — 4B 38
Haarle Rd. SS8: Can I — 6H 39
Haase Cl. CM3: Sth F — 2E 38
Hackamore SS7: Thun — 7H 19
Hacks Dr. SS7: Thun — 5H 19
Haddon Cl. SS6: Ray — 7E 10
Haddon Mead CM3: Sth F — 5H 7
Hadfield Rd. SS17: Stan H — 6D 36
HADLEIGH — 2A 30
Hadleigh Castle (remains of) — 4K 29
Hadleigh Farm & Rare Breeds Cen.
  — 4K 29
Hadleigh Hall Ct. SS9: Lgh S — 4E 30
  (off Hadleigh Rd.)
Hadleigh Pk. — 4H 29
Hadleigh Pk. Av. SS7: Hadl'gh — 2J 29
Hadleigh Pk. Vis. Cen. — 3J 29
Hadleigh Rd. SS0: Wclf S — 6C 32
  SS9: Lgh S — 4E 30
Hainault Av. SS0: Wclf S — 3B 32
  SS4: R'fd — 7J 13
Hainault Cl. SS7: Hadl'gh — 1A 30
Halcyon Rd. SS5: Hull — 6K 7
Hale Way SS3: Shoe — 6F 35
Hallam Ct. CM12: Bill — 3D 4
Hall Cl. SS17: Stan H — 3E 36
Hall Cres. SS7: Hadl'gh — 2K 29
Hallet Rd. SS8: Can I — 5J 39
Hall Farm Cl. SS7: Ben — 4D 28
Hall Farm Rd. SS7: Ben — 3D 28
Hallowell Down CM3: Sth F — 4J 7
Hall Pk. Av. SS0: Wclf S — 5K 31
Hall Pk. Way SS0: Wclf S — 5K 31
Hall Rd. CM0: Ashel — 2K 41
  CM0: S'min — 5H 41
  SS4: R'fd — 3K 21
  SS5: Hawk — 1J 21
Hall Rd. Ind. Est. CM0: S'min — 6H 41
Halstead Cl. SS12: Wick — 5G 9
Halstead Ct. SS12: Wick — 6E 8
Halston Ct. SS17: Corr — 3H 37
Halstow Way SS13: Pit — 7G 17
Haltwhistle Rd. CM3: Sth F — 2G 7
Halyard Reach CM3: Sth F — 5J 7
Hamberts Rd. CM3: Sth F — 1H 7
Hamble Way CM0: Bur C — 4B 40

Hamboro Gdns. SS9: Lgh S — 4D 30
Hambro Av. SS6: Ray — 7H 11
Hambro Cl. SS6: Ray — 7J 11
Hambro Hill SS6: Ray — 6H 11
Hambro Pde. SS6: Ray — 6H 11
Hamilton Cl. SS9: Lgh S — 3C 30
Hamilton Ct. CM3: Sth F — 4J 7
Hamilton Gdns. SS5: Hock — 4E 12
Hamilton M. SS6: Ray — 1B 20
Hamlet Ct. M. SS0: Wclf S — 4C 32
Hamlet Ct. Rd. SS0: Wclf S — 5B 32
Hamlet Rd. SS1: Sth S — 6D 32
Hamley Cl. SS7: Thun — 6B 18
Hammonds La. CM11: Bill — 6A 4
Hampstead Gdns. SS5: Hock — 4F 13
Hampton Cl. SS2: Sth S — 1C 32
Hampton Ct. SS5: Hock — 5C 12
  SS15: Lain — 4G 15
Hampton Gdns. SS2: Sth S — 1C 32
Hamstel M. SS2: Sth S — 4H 33
Hamstel Rd. SS2: Sth S — 2H 33
Handel Rd. SS8: Can I — 6H 39
Handley Grn. SS15: Lain — 7E 14
Handleys Chase SS15: Bas — 2H 15
Handleys Ct. SS15: Bas — 2H 15
Hannah Cl. SS8: Can I — 2E 38
Hannett Rd. SS8: Can I — 5J 39
Hanningfield Cl. SS6: Ray — 1G 19
Hanover Cl. SS14: Bas — 7C 16
Hanover Dr. SS14: Bas — 6C 16
Hanover M. SS5: Hock — 5D 12
Harberts Way SS6: Ray — 6G 11
Harcourt Av. SS2: Sth S — 4D 32
Harcourt Ho. SS2: Sth S — 4D 32
Hardie Rd. SS17: Stan H — 5D 36
Hardings Elms Rd.
  CM11: C Hill — 1K 15
Hardings Reach CM0: Bur C — 6D 40
Hardwick Cl. SS6: Ray — 3K 19
Hardwick Ct. SS0: Wclf S — 2C 32
Hardy Cl. SS3: Shoe — 7D 34
Hardy Rd. SS14: Bas — 4C 16
Hardy's Way SS8: Can I — 2D 38
Harebell Cl. CM12: Bill — 3D 4
Hares Chase CM12: Bill — 4D 4
Haresland Cl. SS7: Hadl'gh — 6B 20
Harewood Av. SS4: Ashin — 6J 13
Harlech Cl. SS13: Pit — 7F 17
Harlequin Steps SS1: Sth S — 6G 33
  (off Hawtree Cl.)
Harley St. SS9: Lgh S — 4E 30
Harold Cl. SS2: Sth S — 4G 33
Harold Gdns. SS11: Wick — 2F 9
Haron Cl. SS8: Can I — 5F 39
Harper Way SS6: Ray — 1J 19
Harridge Cl. SS9: Lgh S — 2G 31
Harridge Rd. SS9: Lgh S — 2G 31
Harrier Cl. SS3: Shoe — 3E 34
Harris Cl. SS12: Wick — 6H 9
  SS17: Corr — 3H 37
Harris Ct. SS5: Hock — 6E 12
Harrison Gdns. SS5: Hull — 1H 11
Harrods Ct. CM11: Bill — 5H 5
Harrogate Dr. SS5: Hock — 3F 13
Harrogate Rd. SS5: Hock — 4F 13
Harrow Cl. SS5: Hawk — 6G 13
Harrow Gdns. SS5: Hawk — 6G 13
Harrow Ho. SS15: Lain — 4D 14
Harrow Rd. SS8: Can I — 3F 39
  SS12: Nth B — 2K 17
Hart Cl. SS7: Thun — 6G 19
Hartford Cl. SS6: Ray — 7E 10
Hartford End SS13: Pit — 7E 16
Hartington Pl. SS1: Sth S — 6F 33
Hartington Rd. SS1: Sth S — 6F 33
Hartland Cl. SS9: Lgh S — 5G 21
Hart Rd. SS7: Thun — 6F 19
Harvard Ct. SS3: Shoe — 7F 11
Harvest Cl. CM3: Sth F — 3H 7
Harvest Rd. SS8: Can I — 3F 39
Harvey Bus. Pk. SS13: Bas — 3G 17
Harvey Cl. SS13: Bas — 3F 17
Harvey Rd. SS13: Bas — 2F 17
Haskins SS17: Stan H — 4F 37
Haslemere Rd. SS11: Wick — 1E 8
Hassell Rd. SS8: Can I — 5H 39
Hassenbrook Rd.
  SS17: Stan H — 5E 36
Hastings, The SS11: Wick — 2F 9
Hastings Rd. SS1: Sth S — 5F 33
Hatfield Dr. CM11: Bill — 5H 5
Hatfield Rd. SS6: Ray — 1H 19
Hatherley, The SS14: Bas — 5B 16
Hatley Gdns. SS7: Ben — 7B 18
Hatterill SS15: Lain — 6E 14
Havalon Cl. SS14: Bas — 5B 16
Havana Dr. SS6: Ray — 5F 11

Haven, The SS1: Sth S — 6A 34
Haven Cl. SS7: Hadl'gh — 2K 29
  SS8: Can I — 5C 38
  SS16: Vange — 2C 26
Havengore SS13: Pit — 4G 17
Havengore Cl. SS3: Gt W — 1J 35
Havengore Ho. SS9: Lgh S — 4G 31
Haven Plotlands Mus. — 2A 24
Haven Quays SS8: Can I — 7A 38
Haven Ri. CM11: Bill — 7B 4
Haven Rd. SS8: Can I — 7A 38
Havering Cl. SS3: Gt W — 1H 35
HAVERING'S GROVE — 5A 4
Havis Rd. SS17: Stan H — 3E 36
Hawbush Grn. SS13: Bas — 3F 17
Hawkesbury Bush La.
  SS16: Vange — 3J 25
Hawkesbury Cl. SS8: Can I — 6D 38
Hawkesbury Rd. SS8: Can I — 5C 38
Hawk Hill SS11: Bat — 7A 6
Hawkins SS3: Shoe — 6D 34
Hawkins Cl. SS11: Wick — 4H 9
Hawk La. SS11: Bat — 1B 10
Hawkley Meade SS5: Hock — 6E 12
Hawkridge SS3: Shoe — 4C 34
Hawks La. SS5: Hock — 6E 12
Hawksway SS16: Bas — 1K 25
HAWKWELL — 6F 13
Hawkwell Chase SS5: Hawk — 6E 12
Hawkwell Pk. Dr. SS5: Hawk — 6F 13
Hawkwell Rd. SS5: Hock — 5E 12
Hawkwood Cl. CM3: Sth F — 1J 7
Hawthorne Cl. SS5: Hawk — 6F 13
Hawthorne Gdns. SS5: Hock — 5B 12
Hawthorn Rd. SS17: Corr — 3F 37
Hawthorn Rd. SS8: Can I — 5G 39
Hawthorns SS7: Ben — 1C 28
Hawthorns, The CM0: Bur C — 3B 40
  CM0: S'min — 5G 41
  SS7: Hadl'gh — 3A 30
  SS17: Corr — 3J 37
Hawthorn Wlk. CM3: Sth F — 1J 7
Hawtree Cl. SS1: Sth S — 6G 33
Hayes Barton SS1: Sth S — 4C 34
Hayes Chase SS11: Bat — 5D 6
Hayes Farm Cvn. Pk.
  SS11: Bat — 6E 6
Hayes La. SS8: Can I — 5D 38
Hayling Gro. SS12: Wick — 6J 9
Hayrick Cl. SS16: Lan H — 1C 24
Hazel Cl. SS7: Hadl'gh — 3B 30
  SS9: Lgh S — 3E 30
  SS15: Bas — 2H 15
Hazeldene SS6: Ray — 7H 11
Hazelmere Rd. SS13: Pit — 1E 26
Hazelwood SS5: Hawk — 7F 13
  SS7: Thun — 5B 18
Hazelwood Gro. SS9: Lgh S — 7G 21
Hazlemere Rd. SS7: Thun — 7D 18
Headcorn Cl. SS13: Pit — 7G 17
Headingley Cl. SS13: Bas — 2E 16
Headley Rd. CM11: Bill — 3G 5
Hearsall Av. SS17: Stan H — 5E 36
Heath Cl. CM12: Bill — 6D 4
Heath Bank CM11: Bill — 5G 5
Heather Cl. SS8: Can I — 6D 38
Heathercroft SS11: Wick — 5J 9
Heather Dr. SS7: Hadl'gh — 3C 30
Heathfield SS6: Ray — 3K 19
  SS7: Thun — 6J 19
Heathfield Ho. SS1: Sth S — 6D 32
  (off Westcliff Pde.)
Heathleigh Dr. SS16: Lan H — 1D 24
Heath Rd. CM11: Ram H — 3J 5
Hedgehope Av. SS6: Ray — 7H 11
Hedge La. SS7: Hadl'gh — 1K 29
Hedgerow, The SS16: Vange — 1B 26
Hedingham Dr. SS12: Wick — 5H 9
Hedingham Pl. SS4: R'fd — 7K 13
Heeswyk Rd. SS2: Sth S — 3H 39
Heideburg Rd. SS8: Can I — 3H 39
Heilsborg Rd. SS8: Can I — 3H 39
Helden Av. SS8: Can I — 3F 39
Helena Cl. SS5: Hawk — 6F 13
Helena Rd. SS6: Ray — 2A 20
Hellendoorn Rd. SS8: Can I — 6H 39
Helmore Ct. SS15: Lain — 6B 14
Helmores SS15: Lain — 6B 14
Helmsdale SS8: Can I — 3D 38
Helmsley Pl. SS14: Bas — 6B 16
Helmshill SS13: Pit — 7F 17
Helpeston SS14: Bas — 6B 16
Hemmells SS14: Bas — 4D 14
Hemmells Pk. SS15: Lain — 3D 14

Hempstalls SS15: Lain — 7H 15
Henderson Gdns. SS12: Wick — 6G 9
Hendon Cl. SS12: Wick — 5F 9
Hengist Gdns. SS11: Wick — 2F 9
Henham Cl. CM11: Bill — 5H 5
Henley Cl. SS5: Hock — 1B 12
Henley Cres. SS0: Wclf S — 1B 32
Henry Dr. SS9: Lgh S — 3C 30
Henson Av. SS8: Can I — 5J 39
Hera Cl. SS2: Sth S — 5J 33
Heralds Way CM3: Sth F — 3J 7
Herbert Gro. SS1: Sth S — 6F 33
Herbert Rd. SS3: Shoe — 6C 34
  SS8: Can I — 4G 39
Herd La. SS17: Corr — 3J 37
Hereford Wlk. SS14: Bas — 5D 16
Hereward Gdns. SS11: Wick — 2F 9
Heritage Way SS4: R'fd — 2C 22
Hermes Dr. CM0: Bur C — 5C 40
Hermes Way SS3: Shoe — 4F 35
Hermitage Av. SS7: Thun — 1G 29
Hermitage Cl. SS7: Thun — 1G 29
Hermitage Dr. SS15: Lain — 6E 14
Hermitage Rd. SS0: Wclf S — 5C 32
Hernen Rd. SS8: Can I — 3G 39
Heron Av. SS11: Wick — 5H 9
Heron Cl. SS6: Ray — 2H 19
Heron Dale SS13: Bas — 6B 16
Heron Gdns. SS6: Ray — 1H 19
Herongate SS3: Shoe — 4E 34
  SS7: Ben — 1B 28
Herons Ga. Trad. Est.
  SS14: Bas — 2E 16
Herschell Ct. SS14: Bas — 5C 16
  (off Nightingale Gro.)
Herschell Rd. SS9: Lgh S — 3E 30
Hertford Dr. SS17: Fob — 4A 26
Hertford Rd. SS8: Can I — 5D 38
Hester Pl. CM0: Bur C — 5D 40
Hetzand Rd. SS3: Shoe — 5K 39
Heybridge Dr. SS12: Wick — 4G 9
Heycroft Rd. SS5: Hawk — 6F 13
  SS9: Lgh S — 6H 21
Heygate Av. SS1: Sth S — 6E 32
Hickling Cl. SS9: Lgh S — 6D 20
Hickstars La. CM12: Bill — 6A 4
Highams Rd. SS5: Hock — 6E 12
High Bank SS16: Lan H — 1B 24
Highbank SS5: Hull — 6J 7
Highbank Cl. SS9: Lgh S — 7H 21
High Barrets SS14: Bas — 7E 16
High Beeches SS7: Ben — 2B 28
Highcliff Cres. SS4: Ashin — 4K 13
High Cliff Dr. SS9: Lgh S — 5H 31
Highcliffe Cl. SS11: Wick — 3H 9
Highcliffe Dr. SS12: Wick — 3B 8
Highcliffe Rd. SS11: Wick — 4H 9
Highcliffe Way SS11: Wick — 4H 9
Highcliff Rd. SS7: Ben — 4E 28
High Cloister CM11: Bill — 5F 5
High Elms Rd. SS5: Hull — 2J 11
Highfield SS5: Hull — 7J 7
Highfield App. CM11: Bill — 7H 5
Highfield Av. SS7: Thun — 1H 29
Highfield Cloisters
  SS9: Lgh S — 4E 30
  (off Hadleigh Rd.)
Highfield Cl. SS0: Wclf S — 3B 32
Highfield Cres. SS0: Wclf S — 3B 32
  SS6: Ray — 2K 19
Highfield Dr. SS0: Wclf S — 2B 32
Highfield Gdns. SS0: Wclf S — 2B 32
Highfield Gro. SS0: Wclf S — 2B 32
Highfield Way CM11: Bill — 2B 32
Highland Gro. CM11: Bill — 5F 5
Highland Rd. SS16: Vange — 3K 25
  SS17: Fob — 4K 25
Highlands Av. SS16: Vange — 1B 26
Highlands Blvd. SS9: Lgh S — 2C 30
Highlands Cres. SS9: Lgh S — 3D 30
Highlands Cres. SS8: B Gif — 6K 17
Highlands Rd. SS11: Raw — 1F 11
  SS13: B Gif — 6K 17
High Mead SS5: Hawk — 6E 12
Highmead SS6: Ray — 2H 19
Highmead Ct. SS6: Ray — 2H 19
High Mdw. CM11: Bill — 5G 5
High Oaks SS16: Lan H — 2D 24
High Pavement SS14: Bas — 6J 15
High Rd. SS5: Hock, Ray — 7A 12
  SS6: Ray — 4J 19
  SS7: Ben — 7B 18
  SS13: Pit — 7F 17
  SS15: Lain — 5D 14
  SS16: Lan H — 1D 24
  SS16: Pit, Vange — 1D 26

High Rd.—Kenholme

High Rd. SS17: Corr, Stan H 6F **37**
(not continuous)
SS17: Fob 4A **26**
SS17: Horn H 3A **36**
High Rd. Nth. SS15: Lain 3E **14**
High St. CM0: Bur C 6D **40**
CM0: S'min 5G **41**
CM12: Bill 6E **4**
SS1: Sth S 5E **32**
(not continuous)
SS3: Gt W 1F **35**
SS3: Shoe 6F **35**
SS6: Ray 2J **19**
SS7: Ben 4D **28**
SS7: Hadl'gh 2K **29**
SS8: Can I 4G **39**
SS9: Lgh S 5E **30**
SS12: Wick 4F **9**
SS17: Stan H 6C **36**
Highview Av. SS16: Lan H 7B **14**
Highview Rd. SS7: Thun 5G **19**
Highwood Cl. SS9: Lgh S 1H **31**
Hilary Cl. SS4: R'fd 6K **13**
Hilary Cres. SS6: Ray 2A **20**
Hilbery Rd. SS8: Can I 5G **39**
Hildaville Dr. SS0: Wclf S 4A **32**
Hillary Mt. CM12: Bill 6D **4**
Hill Av. SS11: Wick 4H **9**
Hillborough Mans.
SS0: Wclf S 2B **32**
Hillborough Rd. SS0: Wclf S 2B **32**
Hill Cl. SS7: Ben 1E **28**
Hillcrest Av. SS5: Hull 2J **11**
SS16: Lan H 1A **24**
Hillcrest Cl. SS17: Horn H 3A **36**
Hillcrest Rd. CM3: Sth F 3G **7**
SS1: Sth S 5F **33**
SS5: Hock 6E **12**
SS17: Horn H 3A **36**
Hillcrest Vw. SS16: Vange 2B **26**
Hill Farm Cotts. CM11: C Hill 5A **8**
Hillhouse Cl. CM12: Bill 3F **5**
Hillhouse Ct. CM12: Bill 3F **5**
Hillhouse Dr. CM12: Bill 3F **5**
Hill La. SS5: Hawk 6F **13**
Hill Rd. SS2: Sth S 2D **32**
SS7: Ben 2E **28**
Hillsboro Rd. SS4: Ashin 2J **13**
Hillside Av. SS5: Hawk 6F **13**
Hillside Cl. CM11: Bill 6F **5**
Hillside Cotts. SS11: Runw 1J **9**
Hillside Cres. SS9: Lgh S 5J **31**
Hillside Rd. CM0: Bur C 5C **40**
CM0: S'min 5F **41**
CM11: Bill 6F **5**
SS5: Hock 6B **12**
SS7: Ben 4D **28**
SS9: Lgh S 5G **31**
(Leigh Hill)
SS9: Lgh S 4E **20**
(Nore Rd.)
Hill Ter. SS17: Corr 3J **37**
Hilltop Av. SS5: Hull 2J **11**
SS7: Ben 3F **29**
Hilltop Cl. SS6: Ray 3J **19**
Hill Top Ri. SS16: Lan H 1B **24**
Hilltop Rd. SS15: Lain 5F **15**
Hill Vw. Cl. CM0: S'min 5F **41**
Hillview Gdns. SS17: Stan H 2F **37**
Hillview Rd. SS6: Ray 1J **19**
Hillway CM11: Bill 5H **5**
SS0: Wclf S 5J **31**
Hillwood Gro. SS11: Wick 4G **9**
Hilly Rd. SS15: Lain 5F **15**
Hilton Rd. SS8: Can I 3E **38**
Hilton Wlk. SS8: Can I 3E **38**
Hilversum Way SS8: Can I 3F **39**
Hindles Rd. SS8: Can I 4H **39**
Hinguar St. SS3: Shoe 6F **35**
Hither Blakers CM3: Sth F 2H **7**
HMP & YOI Bullwood Hall
SS5: Hock 7B **12**
Hobbiton Hill CM3: Sth F 4G **7**
Hobhouse Rd. SS17: Stan H 3D **36**
Hobleythick La. SS0: Wclf S 2B **32**
HOCKLEY 5E **12**
Hockley Cl. SS14: Bas 6B **16**
Hockley Driving Range **6B 12**
Hockley Grn. SS14: Bas 6C **16**
Hockley Pk. SS5: Hock 1C **12**
Hockley Ri. SS5: Hock 6E **12**
Hockley Rd. SS6: Ray 2K **19**
SS14: Bas 6B **16**
Hockley Station (Rail) 5E **12**
Hockley Woods Local Nature Reserve
7C 12
Hodgson Ct. SS11: Wick 6J **9**
Hodgson Way SS11: Wick 5H **9**
Hogarth Dr. SS3: Shoe 4G **35**
Hogarth Way SS4: Ashin 5J **13**
Holbech Rd. SS14: Bas 4D **16**
Holbek Rd. SS8: Can I 5J **39**
Holbrook Cl. CM3: Sth F 3H **7**
CM11: Bill 5H **5**
Holden Gdns. SS14: Bas 3D **16**
Holden Rd. SS14: Bas 3D **16**
Holden Wlk. SS14: Bas 3D **16**
Hole Haven Cvn. Pk.
SS8: Can I 7A **38**
Holgate SS13: Pit 4G **17**
Holkham Av. CM3: Sth F 5H **7**
Holland Av. SS8: Can I 3B **38**
Holland Rd. SS0: Wclf S 6B **32**
Hollands Wlk. SS16: Vange 3B **26**
Holley Gdns. CM11: Bill 4F **5**
Hollies, The SS17: Stan H 6C **36**
Holly Bank SS16: Lan H 1B **24**
Holly Cl. CM0: Bur C 5C **40**
Holly Ct. CM12: Bill 5E **4**
Hollyford CM11: Bill 2H **5**
(not continuous)
Holly Gro. SS16: Lan H 7B **14**
Hollymead SS17: Corr 3E **36**
Holly Tree Gdns. SS6: Ray 4H **19**
Holly Wlk. SS8: Can I 4D **38**
Hollywood Bowl
Basildon **3K 15**
Holmes Ct. SS8: Can I 4H **39**
Holme Wlk. SS12: Wick 6H **9**
Holmsdale Cl. SS0: Wclf S 2A **32**
Holmswood SS8: Can I 3J **39**
Holst Av. SS15: Lain 4E **14**
Holst Cl. SS17: Stan H 4C **36**
Holsworthy SS3: Shoe 4D **34**
Holt Farm Way SS4: R'fd 7K **13**
Holton Rd. SS6: Ray 3C **20**
SS8: Can I 5K **39**
Holtynge SS7: Ben 1C **28**
Holyoak La. SS5: Hawk 7E **12**
Holyrood Dr. SS0: Wclf S 3K **31**
Homecove Ho. *SS0: Wclf S 6B* ***32***
(off Holland Rd.)
Home Farm Cl. SS3: Gt W 1H **35**
Homefield CM0: S'min 4H **41**
Homefield Cl. CM11: Bill 7B **4**
Homefields Av. SS7: Ben 7B **18**
Homeholly Ho. SS11: Runw 1F **9**
Home Mead SS15: Lain 4D **14**
Home Mdws. CM12: Bill 5E **4**
Homeregal Ho. *SS6: Ray 2K* ***19***
(off Bellingham La.)
Homestead Cl. SS6: Ray 7J **11**
Homestead Ct. SS7: Hadl'gh 2K **29**
Homestead Dr. SS16: Bas 3E **24**
Homestead Gdns.
SS7: Hadl'gh 3K **29**
Homestead Rd. CM11: Ram 3A **8**
SS7: Hadl'gh 3K **29**
SS13: B Gif 5J **17**
Homestead Way SS7: Hadl'gh 3K **29**
Honeypot La. SS14: Bas 5K **15**
(not continuous)
Honiley Av. SS12: Wick 1J **17**
Honington Cl. SS11: Wick 5K **9**
Honiton Rd. SS1: Sth S 5G **33**
Honywood Bus. Pk.
SS14: Bas 2D **16**
Honywood Rd. SS14: Bas 2D **16**
Hood Cl. SS12: Wick 5G **9**
Hooley Dr. SS6: Ray 4G **11**
Hoover Dr. SS15: Lain 6B **14**
Hope Av. SS17: Stan H 2E **36**
Hope Rd. SS7: Ben 4D **28**
SS8: Can I 5H **39**
SS17: Stan H 7D **36**
HOPE'S GREEN 3C **28**
Horace Rd. CM11: Bill 3G **5**
SS1: Sth S 6F **33**
Horkesley Way SS12: Wick 5G **9**
Hornbeams SS7: Thun 4B **18**
Hornbeam Way SS15: Lain 3F **15**
Hornby Av. SS0: Wclf S 7A **22**
Hornby Cl. SS0: Wclf S 7B **22**
Hornchurch Cl. SS11: Wick 5J **9**
HORNDON ON THE HILL 4A **36**
Horndon Rd. SS17: Horn H 6A **36**
Hornet Way CM0: Bur C 5C **40**
Hornsby Sq. SS15: Lain 5A **14**
(not continuous)
Hornsby Way SS15: Lain 5B **14**
Hornsland Rd. SS8: Can I 5J **39**
Horseshoe Barracks
SS3: Shoe 6F **35**
Horseshoe Cl. CM12: Bill 2E **4**
Horseshoe Cres. SS3: Shoe 6F **35**
Horseshoe Lawns SS5: Hull 6J **7**
Horsley Cross SS14: Bas 5K **15**
Hospital Rd. SS3: Shoe 6F **35**
Hovefields Av. SS12: Wick 1H **17**
SS13: Bas 2H **17**
Hovefields Cvn. Site
SS13: Bas 2G **17**
Hovefields Ct. Ind. Est.
SS13: Bas 2H **17**
Hovefields Dr. SS12: Wick 1H **17**
Howard Chase SS14: Bas 4H **15**
Howard Cres. SS13: Pit 7G **17**
Howard Pl. SS8: Can I 6F **39**
Howards Chase SS0: Wclf S 3D **32**
Howards Cl. SS9: Lgh S 3J **31**
Howards Ct. SS0: Wclf S 5C **32**
Howards Way SS8: Can I 4A **38**
SS9: Lgh S 4D **20**
Howell Rd. SS17: Corr, Stan H 1F **37**
Howlett Hgts. SS9: Lgh S 5E **20**
Hudson Ct. *SS9: Lgh S 6G* ***21***
(off Hudson Cres.)
Hudson Cres. SS9: Lgh S 6G **21**
Hudson Rd. SS9: Lgh S 6F **21**
Hudsons Cl. SS17: Stan H 4D **36**
Hudson Way SS8: Can I 2E **38**
HULLBRIDGE 1H **11**
Hullbridge Rd. CM3: Sth F 1G **7**
(not continuous)
SS6: Ray 2H **11**
Humber Cl. SS6: Ray 3J **19**
Hunter Dr. SS12: Wick 6G **9**
Hunters Av. CM12: Bill 6A **4**
Hunters Chase CM13: Hut 5A **4**
Huntingdon Rd. SS1: Sth S 5H **33**
Hunts Mead CM12: Bill 6D **4**
Hurlock Rd. CM11: Bill 5F **5**
Hurricane Cl. SS11: Wick 6K **9**
Hurricane Ho. *SS11: Wick 6J* ***9***
(off Hurricane Way)
Hurricane Way SS11: Wick 6J **9**
Hurst Ho. SS7: Thun 5H **19**
Hurst Way SS9: Lgh S 1H **31**
Hyde, The SS16: Lan H 1E **24**
Hyde Way SS12: Wick 5F **9**
Hydeway SS7: Thun 7F **19**
Hyland Ga. CM11: Bill 7B **4**
Hylands, The SS5: Hock 6D **12**
Hylands Gro. SS9: Lgh S 6G **21**

I

Ian Rd. CM12: Bill 3D **4**
Ibis Ct. *SS14: Bas 4A* ***16***
(off Dunlin Dr.)
Icon, The SS14: Bas 7J **15**
Ilford Trad. Est. SS14: Bas 2C **16**
Ilfracombe Av. SS1: Sth S 5H **33**
SS13: B Gif 7H **17**
Ilfracombe Rd. SS2: Sth S 4G **33**
Ilgars Rd. SS11: Wick 2G **9**
Ilmington Dr. SS13: Bas 3E **16**
Imperial Av. SS0: Wclf S 4K **31**
Imperial Ct. *SS0: Wclf S 6C* ***32***
(off Westcliff Pde.)
Imperial Lodge SS0: Wclf S 4A **32**
Imperial Pk. SS3: Shoe 5E **34**
SS6: Ray 5G **11**
Impulse Leisure
Corringham **3F 37**
Inchbonnie Rd. CM3: Sth F 4G **7**
Ingaway SS16: Bas 7H **15**
Inglefield Rd. SS17: Fob 5K **25**
Ingrave Cl. SS12: Wick 5G **9**
Innes Cl. SS12: Wick 6F **9**
Integra SS12: Wick 4C **8**
International Bus. Pk.
SS8: Can I 5B **38**
Inverness Av. SS0: Wclf S 3B **32**
Invicta Ct. CM12: Bill 4C **4**
Inworth Wlk. SS11: Wick 3J **9**
Iona Way SS12: Wick 5H **9**
Ipswich M. SS16: Lan H 7B **14**
Iris M. SS15: Lain 7E **14**
Ironwell Cl. SS4: R'fd 2C **22**
Ironwell La. SS4: R'fd 2C **22**
SS5: Hawk 1J **21**
Irvine Pl. SS12: Wick 6H **9**
Irvine Way CM12: Bill 6E **4**
Irvington Cl. SS9: Lgh S 1F **31**
Irvon Hill Rd. SS12: Wick 4E **8**
Isabel Evans Ct. SS17: Corr 2F **37**
Ivanhurst Ind. Est. SS11: Bat 6B **6**
Ivy Ga. Cl. SS11: Wick 3G **9**
Ivy Path SS14: Bas 6C **16**
Ivy Rd. SS7: Thun 6A **18**
Ivy Wlk. SS8: Can I 4D **38**

J

Jackdaw Cl. CM11: Bill 7G **5**
SS3: Shoe 4E **34**
Jacks Cl. SS11: Wick 4H **9**
Jacksons La. CM11: Bill 4F **5**
Jacksons M. CM11: Bill 5G **5**
Jacqueline Gdns. CM12: Bill 3F **5**
James Sq. CM11: Bill 5J **5**
Janette Av. SS8: Can I 5C **38**
Jardine Rd. SS13: Pit 4G **17**
Jarvis Rd. SS7: Ben 1E **28**
SS8: Can I 2E **38**
Jasmine Cl. SS8: Can I 6D **38**
SS16: Lan H 1B **24**
Jasmine Ct. SS5: Hock 4E **12**
Jason Cl. SS8: Can I 3F **39**
Jefferies Way SS17: Stan H 4F **37**
Jefferson Av. SS15: Lain 6C **14**
Jena Cl. SS3: Shoe 5E **34**
Jenner Rd. SS14: Bas 5D **16**
Jermayns SS15: Lain 6G **15**
Jersey Gdns. SS11: Wick 3F **9**
Jesmond Rd. SS8: Can I 6F **39**
Jetty M. SS1: Sth S 6H **33**
John Childs Way SS6: Ray 2A **20**
Johnson Cl. SS4: R'fd 6K **13**
SS12: Wick 6F **9**
Johnson Ct. SS4: R'fd 2D **22**
Johnstone Rd. SS1: Sth S 5A **34**
John St. SS3: Shoe 6G **35**
Jones Cl. SS2: Sth S 2C **32**
Jones Cnr. SS9: Lgh S 5F **21**
Jordans, The SS2: Sth S 3E **32**
Jordan Way SS14: Bas 5D **16**
Josselin Ct. SS13: Bas 2G **17**
Josselin Rd. SS13: Bas 2G **17**
Jotmans La. SS7: Ben 3K **27**
Journeymans Way SS2: Sth S 7D **22**
Jubilee Cl. SS5: Hawk 6E **12**
Jubilee Dr. SS11: Wick 3E **8**
Jubilee Pl. SS0: Wclf S 7K **21**
Jubilee Rd. CM11: C Hill 1A **16**
SS6: Ray 2A **20**
Juliers Cl. SS8: Can I 5H **39**
Juliers Rd. SS8: Can I 5H **39**
Junction Rd. SS16: Pit 1F **27**
Juniper Cl. CM11: Bill 3G **5**
Juniper Rd. SS9: Lgh S 1H **31**
Juniper W. SS15: Lain 5B **14**

K

Kale Rd. SS7: Ben 1E **28**
Kamerwyk Av. SS8: Can I 4G **39**
Karen Cl. SS7: Ben 5D **28**
SS12: Wick 5E **8**
SS17: Stan H 5C **36**
Katherine Cl. SS6: Ray 3C **20**
Katherine Rd. SS13: B Gif 5J **17**
Kathleen Cl. SS17: Stan H 3E **36**
Kathleen Dr. SS9: Lgh S 3H **31**
Kathleen Ferrier Cres.
SS15: Lain 4E **14**
Kathryn Ct. *SS3: Shoe 6E* ***34***
(off Avon Way)
Keats Ho. SS2: Sth S 3F **33**
Keats Sq. CM3: Sth F 4J **7**
Keats Wlk. SS6: Ray 2C **20**
Keats Way SS12: Wick 4E **8**
Keegan Pl. SS8: Can I 4G **39**
Keeper's Cotts. CM11: Bill 2J **5**
Keer Av. SS8: Can I 6H **39**
Keighley M. SS3: Shoe 2D **34**
Keith Av. SS11: Runw 2F **9**
Keith Way SS2: Sth S 7C **22**
Kellington Rd. SS8: Can I 3G **39**
(not continuous)
Kelly Rd. SS13: B Gif 6J **17**
Kelso Cl. SS6: Ray 5G **11**
Kelvedon Cl. CM11: Bill 5G **5**
SS6: Ray 1G **19**
Kelvedon Rd. CM11: Bill 5G **5**
Kelvin Rd. SS7: Thun 5D **18**
Kelvinside SS17: Stan H 3E **36**
Kembles SS6: Ray 6J **11**
Kempton Cl. SS7: Thun 5H **19**
Kendal Cl. SS5: Hull 2J **11**
SS6: Ray 2A **20**
Kendal Ct. SS11: Wick 6J **9**
Kendal Way SS9: Lgh S 5G **21**
Kenholme SS9: Lgh S 1G **31**

Kenilworth Cl.—Lesney Gdns.

Kenilworth Cl. CM12: Bill 5C 4
Kenilworth Gdns. SS0: Wclf S 2J 31
SS6: Ray 1H 19
Kenilworth Pl. SS15: Bas 3G 15
Kenley Cl. SS11: Wick 5K 9
Kenmar Cl. SS6: Ray 4C 20
Kenmore Cl. SS8: Can I 6J 39
Kennedy Av. SS15: Lain 6B 14
Kennedy Cl. SS6: Ray 4C 20
SS7: Thun 5B 18
Kennel La. CM11: Bill 6A 4
CM12: Bill 6A 4
Kenneth Gdns. SS17: Stan H 2F 37
Kenneth Rd. SS7: Thun 6F 19
SS13: Pit 5G 17
Kennet Way SS14: Bas 5D 16
Kennington Av. SS7: Thun 7C 18
Kensington Gdns. CM12: Bill 3E 4
Kensington Rd. SS1: Sth S 5H 33
Kensington Way SS5: Hock 5C 12
Kent Av. SS8: Can I 3F 39
SS9: Lgh S 3H 31
Kent Cl. SS15: Lain 6D 14
Kent Elms Cl. SS2: Sth S 7H 21
Kent Grn. Cl. SS5: Hock 6F 13
Kenton Way SS16: Lan H 7B 14
Kents Hill Rd. SS7: Ben 2D 28
Kents Hill Rd. Nth. SS7: Thun 7D 18
Kent Vw. Av. SS9: Lgh S 5J 31
Kent Vw. Ct. SS8: Can I 7F 39
Kent Vw. M. SS16: Vange 7D 16
Kent Vw. Rd. SS16: Vange 7D 16
Kent Way SS6: Ray 4C 20
Kentwell Ct. SS7: Ben 2C 28
Kenway SS2: Sth S 3E 32
Kenway Ct. SS2: Sth S 3E 32
Kenwood Rd. SS17: Corr 3H 37
Kersbrooke Way SS17: Corr 2H 37
Kershaws Cl. SS12: Wick 5E 8
Kestrel Gro. SS6: Ray 1H 19
Kestrel Ho. SS3: Shoe 3F 35
Keswick Av. SS5: Hull 1J 11
Keswick Cl. SS6: Ray 2A 20
Keswick Rd. SS7: Thun 6E 18
Kevin Cl. CM11: Bill 6B 4
Keyes Cl. SS3: Shoe 3E 34
Keysland SS7: Thun 6H 19
Kibcaps SS16: Bas 1H 25
Kierbeck Bus. Pk. SS16: Pit 2D 26
Kilbarry Wlk. CM11: Bill 1H 5
Kiln Rd. SS7: Ben, Thun 1F 29
Kiln Shaw SS16: Lan H 1E 24
Kilnwood Av. SS5: Hock 6D 12
Kilowan Cl. SS16: Lan H 1B 24
Kilworth Av. SS1: Sth S 5F 33
Kimberley Ct. SS7: Ben 2C 28
Kimberley Dr. SS15: Bas 2H 15
Kimberley Rd. SS7: Ben 2C 28
King Edward Av. CM0: Bur C 4C 40
King Edward Mead
SS15: Lain 5D 14
King Edward Rd. SS15: Lain 4D 14
SS17: Stan H 7D 36
King Edward's Rd. CM3: Sth F 2G 7
King Edward Ter. SS15: Lain 5D 14
Kingfisher Cl. SS3: Shoe 3E 34
Kingfisher Cres. SS6: Ray 1H 19
Kingfisher Dr. SS7: Ben 3C 28
Kingfishers SS16: Bas 1A 26
Kingfishers, The SS11: Wick 6H 9
King George's Cl. SS6: Ray 2K 19
King Henry's Dr. SS4: R'fd 5D 22
Kingley Cl. SS12: Wick 4D 8
Kingley Dr. SS12: Wick 4D 8
Kings Cl. SS6: Ray 2A 20
SS8: Can I 5A 38
Kings Ct. CM0: Bur C 6C 40
Kings Cres. SS15: Lain 3D 14
Kings Cft. CM0: S'min 5G 41
Kingsdown Cl. SS13: Pit 6G 17
Kingsdown Wlk. SS8: Can I 3E 38
Kings Farm SS6: Ray 6J 11
Kings Ga. SS6: Ray 1K 19
Kingsgate Ct. SS0: Wclf S 5A 32
Kingshawes SS7: Thun 6H 19
Kingsleigh Pk. Homes
SS7: Thun 6H 19
Kingsley Cres. SS7: Thun 4H 19
Kingsley La. SS7: Thun 4H 19
Kingsley Mdws. SS12: Wick 6F 9
Kings Lodge SS7: Hadl'gh 2J 29
Kingsman Rd. SS17: Stan H 6B 36
Kingsmans Farm Rd. SS5: Hull 6K 7
Kingsmere SS7: Thun 7H 19
Kingsmere Cl. SS8: Can I 4J 39
Kings Pde. *SS17: Stan H* *6C 36*
(off King St.)
Kings Pk. SS7: Thun 7F 19
SS8: Can I 4J 39
Kings Pl. CM0: S'min 5G 41
King's Rd. SS0: Wclf S 4J 31
SS7: Ben 3E 28
Kings Rd. CM0: Bur C 6C 40
CM0: S'min 6G 41
SS6: Ray 2A 20
SS8: Can I 5A 38
SS15: Lain 3D 14
Kingsteignton SS3: Shoe 3C 34
Kingston Av. SS3: Shoe 2E 34
Kingston Hill SS16: Bas 3F 25
Kingston Ridge SS16: Bas 3F 25
Kingston Rd. SS7: Thun 1H 29
Kingston Way SS7: Thun 6F 19
SS16: Bas 2G 25
King St. SS17: Stan H 6C 36
Kingsview Ct. SS11: Wick 5H 9
Kings Way CM3: Sth F 1G 7
CM11: Bill 7B 4
Kingsway SS0: Wclf S 3J 31
SS5: Hull 2H 11
Kingsway M. SS0: Wclf S 3K 31
KINGSWOOD 1K 25
Kingswood Chase
SS9: Lgh S 2F 31
Kingswood Cl. CM11: Bill 5G 5
Kingswood Ct. SS16: Vange 7C 16
Kingswood Cres. SS6: Ray 3H 19
Kingswood M. SS6: Ray 3H 19
Kingswood Rd. SS16: Bas 7A 16
Kipling M. SS2: Sth S 3E 32
Kirby Rd. SS14: Bas 6C 16
Kirkham Av. SS17: Horn H 6B 24
Kirkham Rd. SS17: Horn H 6B 24
Kirkham Shaw SS17: Horn H 5B 24
Kitkatts Rd. SS8: Can I 5E 38
(not continuous)
Knares, The SS16: Bas 1G 25
Knightbridge Wlk. CM12: Bill 4E 4
Knights SS15: Lain 5F 15
Knight's Ct. SS14: Bas 4D 16
Knight St. CM3: Sth F 3J 7
Knightswick Cen.
SS8: Can I 4G 39
Knightswick Rd. SS8: Can I 4F 39
Knivet Cl. SS6: Ray 3A 20
Knole Cl. CM3: Sth F 5H 7
Knoll, The CM12: Bill 3F 5
SS6: Ray 2K 19
Knollcroft SS3: Shoe 7D 34
Knowle, The SS16: Vange 1A 26
Knox Ct. SS12: Wick 6H 9
Kolburg Rd. SS8: Can I 6H 39
Kollum Rd. SS8: Can I 5K 39
Koln Cl. SS8: Can I 5A 38
Komberg Cres. SS8: Can I 3G 39
Konnybrook SS7: Thun 1G 29
Korndyk Av. SS8: Can I 4G 39
Kursaal SS1: Sth S 6G 33
Kursaal Pavement *SS1: Sth S* *6G 33*
(off Southchurch Av.)
Kursaal Way SS1: Sth S 6G 33
Kynoch Ct. SS17: Stan H 6E 36

L

Laars Av. SS8: Can I 4G 39
Laburnum Av. SS12: Wick 5E 8
Laburnum Cl. SS5: Hock 5C 12
SS12: Wick 5E 8
Laburnum Dr. SS17: Corr 3H 37
Laburnum Gro. SS5: Hock 5B 12
SS8: Can I 5B 38
Laburnum Way SS6: Ray 5F 11
Labworth La. SS8: Can I 6G 39
(not continuous)
Labworth Rd. SS8: Can I 6G 39
Ladram Cl. SS1: Sth S 4C 34
Ladram Rd. SS1: Sth S 3B 34
Ladram Way SS1: Sth S 4B 34
Ladygate Cen. SS12: Wick 4F 9
Lady Hamilton Ct. SS1: Sth S 4B 34
Ladysmith Way SS15: Bas 2H 15
LAINDON 6D 14
Laindon Cen. SS15: Lain 6D 14
Laindon Link SS15: Lain 6E 14
Laindon Rd. CM12: Bill 6E 4
SS17: Horn H 7B 24
Laindon Station (Rail) 7E 14
Lake Av. CM12: Bill 4E 4
Lake Dr. SS7: Thun 7E 18
Lake Mdw. SS8: Can I 4J 39
Lake Mdws. Bus. Pk.
CM12: Bill 4D 4
Lakenham Ho. *SS2: Sth S* *7C 22*
(off Manners Way)
Lakeside CM12: Bill 3E 4
SS6: Ray 7H 11
Lakeside Cres. SS8: Can I 3H 39
Lakeside Path SS8: Can I 3E 38
Lake Vw. SS16: Lan H 1B 24
Lakeview SS8: Can I 3E 38
(Hilton Rd.)
SS8: Can I 4H 39
(Kings Pk.)
Lambeth M. SS5: Hock 5C 12
Lambeth Rd. SS7: Thun 6C 18
SS9: Lgh S 6G 21
Lambourn Cl. SS3: Shoe 2E 34
Lambourne SS8: Can I 6E 38
Lambourne Cres. SS14: Bas 7D 16
Lamont Cl. SS12: Wick 6G 9
Lampern Cl. CM12: Bill 1F 5
Lampern Cres. CM12: Bill 1F 5
Lampern M. CM12: Bill 1F 5
Lampetsdowne SS17: Corr 3H 37
Lampits Hill SS17: Corr 1G 37
Lampits Hill Av. SS17: Corr 2G 37
Lampits La. SS17: Corr 2G 37
Lancaster Cres. *SS1: Sth S* *5F 33*
(off Lancaster Gdns.)
Lancaster Dr. SS16: Lan H 7B 14
Lancaster Gdns. SS1: Sth S 5F 33
SS6: Ray 4C 20
Lancaster Rd. SS6: Ray 4C 20
Lancer Way CM12: Bill 4D 4
Landermere SS14: Bas 5K 15
Landsburg Rd. SS8: Can I 3H 39
Landwick Cotts. SS3: Gt W 1K 35
Langdon Bus. Cen.
SS16: Lan H 7E 14
LANGDON HILLS 1D 24
Langdon Hills Country Pk. 5D 24
Langdon Hills Golf Course 5A 24
Langdon M. CM11: Bill 4F 5
Langdon Nature Reserve
Lower Dunton Rd. 2B 24
Staneway 1E 24
Langdon Rd. SS6: Ray 1H 19
Langdon Visitor Cen. 2A 24
Langdon Way SS17: Corr 2H 37
Langemore Way CM11: Bill 6F 5
Langenhoe SS12: Wick 5G 9
Langford Cres. SS7: Thun 6F 19
Langford Gro. SS13: Bas 4G 17
Langham Cres. CM12: Bill 7F 5
Langham Dr. SS6: Ray 1G 19
Langland Cl. SS17: Corr 3G 37
Langley Cl. SS9: Lgh S 5D 20
Langley Pl. CM12: Bill 4C 4
Langleys SS16: Bas 1K 25
Langport Dr. SS0: Wclf S 1J 31
Langside Cl. SS15: Lain 4D 14
Langthorns CM12: Bill 5F 5
Lanham Pl. SS13: Bas 4F 17
Lanhams SS13: Pit 4F 17
Lanhams Ct. SS13: Pit 4F 17
Lansdown Av. SS7: Hadl'gh 6B 20
Lansdowne Av. SS9: Lgh S 4J 31
Lansdowne Dr. SS6: Ray 1H 19
Lantern Ter. *SS1: Sth S* *6G 33*
(off Hawtree Cl.)
Lappmark Rd. SS8: Can I 5H 39
Lapwater Cl. SS9: Lgh S 4E 30
Lapwater Ct. *SS9: Lgh S* *3E 30*
(off London Rd.)
Lapwing Path *SS14: Bas* *4A 16*
(off Dunlin Dr.)
Lapwing Rd. SS11: Wick 1E 8
Larch Cl. SS15: Lain 3E 14
Larches, The SS7: Thun 4C 18
Larchwood Cl. SS9: Lgh S 6D 20
Larke Ri. SS2: Sth S 1B 32
Larkfield SS17: Corr 2H 37
Larkfield Cl. SS4: R'fd 7K 13
Larkspur Way SS15: Lain 7E 14
Larkswood Rd. SS17: Corr 2H 37
Larkswood Wlk. SS12: Wick 5F 9
Lark Way SS14: Bas 5D 16
Larmarsh Path SS14: Bas 4D 16
Larup Av. SS8: Can I 4G 39
Larup Gdns. SS8: Can I 4G 39
Lascelles Gdns. SS4: Ashin 6J 13
Latchetts Shaw SS16: Bas 1K 25
Latchingdon Cl. SS6: Ray 1G 19
Latimer Dr. SS15: Lain 3D 14
Laurel Av. SS12: Wick 4E 8
Laurel Cl. SS9: Lgh S 5F 31
Laurel Ct. SS4: R'fd 7J 13
Laurels, The CM3: Sth F 2H 7
SS6: Ray 4B 20
Laurence Ind. Est. SS2: Sth S 6K 21
Lauriston Pl. *SS1: Sth S* *5F 33*
(off Southchurch Av.)
Lavender Dr. CM0: S'min 6F 41
Lavender Gro. SS0: Wclf S 2B 32
Lavender M. SS0: Wclf S 2B 32
SS8: Can I 6D 38
SS17: Stan H 4E 36
Lavender Way SS12: Wick 4E 8
Lavers, The SS6: Ray 1A 20
Lawn Av. SS2: Sth S 3F 33
Lawns, The SS7: Thun 5C 18
Lawns Ct. SS7: Thun 5B 18
Lawrence Rd. SS13: B Gif 4K 17
Laxtons SS17: Stan H 4D 36
Laxtons, The SS4: Ashin 6K 13
Leamington Rd. SS1: Sth S 5G 33
SS5: Hock 4F 13
Lea Rd. SS7: Ben 7C 18
Leas, The CM0: Bur C 4D 40
SS0: Wclf S 6A 32
Leas Cl. SS0: Wclf S 5K 31
Leas Ct. CM0: Bur C 4D 40
Leas Gdns. SS0: Wclf S 5K 31
Leaside SS7: Thun 6B 18
Leasway SS0: Wclf S 5K 31
SS6: Ray 2J 19
SS12: Wick 5D 8
Leather La. SS1: Sth S 5E 32
Leaway CM12: Bill 7F 5
Lectern M. SS15: Lain 6F 15
Lede Rd. SS8: Can I 4F 39
Lee Chapel La. SS16: Bas 2E 24
LEE CHAPEL NORTH 6G 15
LEE CHAPEL SOUTH 1H 25
Leecon Way SS4: R'fd 1B 22
Lee Lotts SS3: Gt W 1G 35
Lee Rd. SS13: B Gif 6K 17
Lee Wlk. SS16: Bas 7G 15
Leeward Rd. CM3: Sth F 5J 7
Lee Woottens La. SS16: Bas 7J 15
(not continuous)
Leicester Av. SS4: R'fd 4D 22
Leige Av. SS8: Can I 2E 38
Leigham Ct. Dr. SS9: Lgh S 4H 31
LEIGH BECK 5J 39
Leigh Beck La. SS8: Can I 6J 39
Leigh Beck Rd. SS8: Can I 5K 39
Leigh Cliff Rd. SS9: Lgh S 5H 31
Leighcroft Gdns. SS9: Lgh S 1F 31
Leigh Fells SS13: Pit 6G 17
Leighfields SS7: Thun 6H 19
Leighfields Av. SS9: Lgh S 6F 21
Leighfields Rd. SS9: Lgh S 6F 21
Leigh Gdns. SS9: Lgh S 4E 30
Leigh Golf Driving Range 5C 30
Leigh Hall Rd. SS9: Lgh S 4G 31
Leigh Heath Ct. SS9: Lgh S 3C 30
Leigh Hgts. SS7: Hadl'gh 2B 30
Leigh Heritage Cen. 5F 31
Leigh Hill SS9: Lgh S 5G 31
Leigh Hill Cl. SS9: Lgh S 5G 31
Leigh Ho. SS9: Lgh S 5G 31
Leighlands Rd. CM3: Sth F 3H 7
Leigh National Nature Reserve
6D 30
LEIGH-ON-SEA 4G 31
Leigh-on-Sea Sailing Club 5G 31
Leigh-on-Sea Station (Rail) 5E 30
Leigh Pk. Cl. SS9: Lgh S 4E 30
Leigh Pk. Rd. SS9: Lgh S 5F 31
Leigh Rd. SS8: Can I 6F 39
SS9: Lgh S 4H 31
Leighs Rifleman CM12: Bill 4C 4
Leighton Av. SS9: Lgh S 4H 31
Leighton Rd. SS7: Thun 5C 18
Leigh Vw. Dr. SS9: Lgh S 1G 31
Leighville Gro. SS9: Lgh S 4F 31
Leighwood Av. SS9: Lgh S 7F 21
Leinster Rd. SS15: Lain 5E 14
Leisure Island Fun Pk. 7G 39
Leitrim Av. SS3: Shoe 6C 34
Lekoe Rd. SS8: Can I 2D 38
Lenham Way SS13: Pit 6G 17
Lennon Cres. SS14: Bas 5D 16
Lennox Dr. SS12: Wick 6H 9
Leonard Dr. SS6: Ray 7E 10
Leonard M. SS17: Stan H 2E 36
Leonard Rd. SS0: Wclf S 5B 32
SS16: Vange 3K 25
Leon Dr. SS16: Vange 2B 26
Leslie Cl. SS9: Lgh S 6F 21
Leslie Dr. SS9: Lgh S 6F 21
Leslie Gdns. SS6: Ray 3B 20
Leslie Pk. CM0: Bur C 6D 40
Leslie Rd. SS6: Ray 3A 20
Lesney Gdns. SS4: R'fd 1B 22

A-Z Southend-on-Sea 53

Lettons Chase—Maplin Ct.

Lettons Chase CM3: Sth F 4H 7
Letzen Rd. SS8: Can I 4E 38
Leveller Row CM12: Bill 4D 4
Lever La. SS4: R'fd 3D 22
Levett Rd. SS17: Stan H 5E 36
Lewes Rd. SS2: Sth S 2G 33
Lewes Way SS7: Thun 5H 19
Leyd Rd. SS8: Can I 4F 39
Leyland Ct. SS1: Sth S 5F 33
Leys, The SS16: Vange 1A 26
Leysings SS16: Bas 1G 25
Lichfields, The SS14: Bas 5D 16
Liddell Dr. SS14: Bas 3D 16
Lifstan Wlk. SS2: Sth S 5J 33
Lifstan Way SS1: Sth S 5J 33
Lilac Av. SS8: Can I 4G 39
SS12: Wick 5E 8
Lilford Rd. CM11: Bill 3G 5
Lilian Pl. SS6: Ray 4C 20
Lilian Rd. CM0: Bur C 5C 40
Lilyville Wlk. SS6: Ray 3C 20
Limburg Rd. SS8: Can I 4B 38
Lime Av. SS9: Lgh S 3E 30
Lime Ct. SS5: Hock 5E 12
Lime Lodge SS9: Lgh S 3E 30
Lime Pl. SS15: Lain 3E 14
Lime Rd. SS7: Ben 1E 28
Limes, The SS6: Ray 4B 20
Limeslade Cl. SS17: Corr 3G 37
Limetree Av. SS7: Ben 1B 28
Limetree Rd. SS8: Can I 4J 39
Lime Way CM0: Bur C 4B 40
Lincefield SS16: Lan H 2D 24
Lincewood Pk. Dr.
SS16: Lan H 1C 24
Lincoln Chase SS2: Sth S 2J 33
Lincoln Cl. SS2: Sth S 2J 33
Lincoln Rd. SS4: Ashin 5H 13
SS14: Bas 5D 16
Lincoln Way SS6: Ray 6G 11
SS8: Can I 4C 38
Linda Gdns. CM12: Bill 3C 4
Linden Cl. SS6: Ray 3B 20
SS7: Thun 6C 18
Linden Ct. SS7: Thun 6C 18
SS9: Lgh S 3J 31
(off London Rd.)
Linden Leas SS7: Thun 6C 18
Linden Rd. SS7: Thun 7C 18
Lindens, The SS16: Lan H 7C 14
Linden Way SS8: Can I 4D 38
Linde Rd. SS8: Can I 4F 39
Lindisfarne Av. SS9: Lgh S 3J 31
Lindisfarne Ct. SS12: Wick 6J 9
Lindon Rd. SS11: Runw 1E 8
Lindsell Grn. SS14: Bas 7C 16
Lindsell La. SS14: Bas 7C 16
Lindsey Ct. SS6: Ray 1G 19
SS12: Wick 6G 9
Lindsey Rd. SS3: Gt W 1H 35
Linford Dr. SS14: Bas 6C 16
Lingcroft SS16: Bas 1J 25
Lingfield Dr. SS4: R'fd 2E 22
Linkdale CM12: Bill 7F 5
Link Rd. SS6: Ray 1K 19
SS8: Can I 5C 38
SS17: Stan H 4D 36
Links, The CM12: Bill 3C 4
Links Ct. SS1: Sth S 6J 33
(not continuous)
Links Way SS7: Hadl'gh 2B 30
Linksway SS9: Lgh S 1E 30
Linkway SS14: Bas 6K 15
Linne Rd. SS8: Can I 3G 39
Linnet Cl. SS3: Shoe 4E 34
Linnet Dr. SS7: Ben 3C 28
Linnets SS16: Bas 2J 25
Linroping Av. SS8: Can I 5K 39
Linton Rd. SS3: Shoe 6E 34
Lionel Rd. SS8: Can I 5E 38
Lion Hill SS17: Fob 3K 37
Lion La. CM12: Bill 5E 4
Lippits Hill SS16: Lan H 2E 24
Lisa Cl. CM12: Bill 1F 5
Little Bentley SS14: Bas 5K 15
Lit. Berry La. SS16: Lan H 1C 24
Littlebury Ct. SS13: Bas 4E 16
Littlebury Grn. SS13: Bas 4E 16
Little Charlton SS13: Pit 6G 17
Little Chittock SS14: Bas 6C 16
Littlecroft CM3: Sth F 4H 7
Little Dodden SS16: Bas 1H 25
Little Fretches SS9: Lgh S 1G 31
Little Garth SS13: Pit 7E 16
Lit. Gypps Cl. SS8: Can I 4D 38
Lit. Gypps Ct. SS8: Can I 4D 38
Lit. Gypps Rd. SS8: Can I 5D 38
Little Haven Nature Reserve 5K 19
LITTLE HAVENS CHILDREN'S HOSPICE 5K 19
Little Hays SS9: Lgh S 6D 20
Littlehurst La. SS15: Bas 2H 15
Little Kingston SS16: Bas 3F 25
Little Lullaway SS15: Lain 5G 15
Lit. Malgraves Ind. Est.
RM14: Bulp 4B 24
Lit. Norsey Rd. CM11: Bill 3G 5
Lit. Oak M. SS11: Wick 4F 9
Little Oaks SS14: Bas 6J 15
Little Oxcroft SS15: Lain 6D 14
Little Searles SS13: Pit 5F 17
Little Spenders SS14: Bas 4B 16
Lit. Stambridge Hall La.
SS4: R'fd 2F 23
Little Thorpe SS1: Sth S 3A 34
SS16: Vange 1D 26
Lit. Wakering Hall La.
SS3: Gt W 1G 35
Lit. Wakering Rd.
SS3: Barl M, L Wak, Gt W 1F 35
Lit. Wheatley Chase
SS6: Ray 1G 19
Lloyd Wise Cl. SS2: Sth S 2H 33
Locarno Av. SS11: Runw 2G 9
Locke Cl. SS17: Stan H 4C 36
Locks Hill SS4: R'fd 3D 22
Locksley Cl. SS2: Sth S 3K 33
Lodge Cl. SS6: Ray 3A 20
SS7: Thun 7G 19
Lodge Farm Cl. SS9: Lgh S 7F 21
Lodgelands Cl. SS6: Ray 3B 20
Lodwick SS3: Shoe 7C 34
Logan Link SS12: Wick 6H 9
Lombardy Cl. SS13: Pit 6G 17
London Gateway Logistics Pk.
SS17: Stan H 6K 37
London Hill SS6: Ray 1K 19
London M. SS12: Wick 4D 8
London Rd. CM11: C Hill, Ram 5A 8
CM12: Bill 5B 4
SS0: Wclf S 4A 32
SS1: Sth S 5D 32
SS6: Ray 6B 10
SS7: Ben, Thun 7B 18
SS7: Hadl'gh, Lgh S 2J 29
SS9: Lgh S, Sth S, Wclf S
3E 30
SS11: Raw 4K 9
(Crouchview Cl.)
SS11: Raw 6B 10
(Old London Rd.)
SS12: Wick 5A 8
SS13: B Gif, Pit 7G 17
SS16: Vange 3A 26
SS17: Stan H 6B 36
London Rd. Retail Pk.
SS2: Sth S 4D 32
LONDON SOUTHEND AIRPORT
5C 22
Long Acre SS14: Bas 6A 16
Longborough Cl. SS13: Bas 3E 16
Longbow SS2: Sth S 3J 33
Longfield Cl. SS11: Wick 4J 9
Longfield Rd. CM3: Sth F 2H 7
SS11: Wick 4J 9
Long Gages SS14: Bas 5K 15
(not continuous)
Longhams Dr. CM3: Sth F 2H 7
Long La. SS5: Hull 2K 11
Long Lynderswood
SS15: Lain 6H 15
Longmans *SS3: Shoe 6G 35*
(off Rampart St.)
Longmead SS13: Pit 4G 17
Long Mdw. CM12: Bill 3E 4
(not continuous)
Long Meadow Dr. SS11: Wick 3G 9
Long Riding SS14: Bas 6K 15
(not continuous)
Longrise CM12: Bill 7F 5
Long Rd. SS8: Can I 5C 38
Longsand SS3: Shoe 5D 34
Longtail CM11: Bill 2G 5
Long Vw. SS8: Can I 4D 38
Longwick SS16: Lan H 1E 24
Lonsdale Ct. SS2: Sth S 2H 33
Lonsdale Rd. SS2: Sth S 3H 33
Lord Roberts Av. SS9: Lgh S 4H 31
Lords Ct. SS13: Bas 1F 17
Lords Way SS13: Bas 2F 17
Lorien Gdns. CM3: Sth F 4G 7
Lornes Cl. SS2: Sth S 2H 33
Lorraine Cl. CM11: Bill 7B 4
Lorrimore Cl. CM12: Bill 2D 4
Loten Rd. SS7: Ben 3B 28
Lottem Rd. SS8: Can I 6H 39
Louisa Av. SS7: Thun 6B 18
Louis Cl. SS6: Ray 1G 19
Louis Dr. SS6: Ray 7E 10
Louis Dr. E. SS6: Ray 1H 19
Louis Dr. W. SS6: Ray 7E 10
Louise Rd. SS6: Ray 2A 20
Louvaine Av. SS12: Wick 3D 8
Lovelace Av. SS1: Sth S 5H 33
Lovelace Gdns. SS2: Sth S 4H 33
Love La. SS6: Ray 2J 19
Lovell Ri. SS9: Lgh S 6J 21
Lovens Cl. SS8: Can I 6G 39
Lower Av. SS13: B Gif 3J 17
Lwr. Church Rd. SS7: Thun 6B 18
Lower Cloister CM11: Bill 5F 5
Lwr. Dunton Rd. CM13: Dun 7A 14
RM14: Bulp 3A 24
SS17: Horn H 3A 24
Lower Lambricks SS6: Ray 7H 11
Lower Pk. Rd. SS12: Wick 7E 8
Lower Rd. SS5: Hock, Hull 2K 11
SS5: Hull 2H 11
Lwr. Southend Rd.
SS11: Wick 3F 9
Lower St. SS15: Bas 3G 15
Low Rd. SS3: Shoe 7E 34
Lowry Cl. SS3: Shoe 3F 35
Loxford SS13: Bas 4E 16
Lubbards Cl. SS6: Ray 6H 11
Lucam Lodge SS4: R'fd 3D 22
Lucerne Dr. SS11: Wick 4J 9
Lucerne Wlk. SS11: Wick 4J 9
Luckyn La. SS14: Bas 4H 15
Lucy Rd. SS1: Sth S 6F 33
Ludlow M. SS13: Pit 6F 17
Luker Rd. SS1: Sth S 5E 32
Lulworth Cl. SS17: Stan H 7B 36
Luncies Rd. SS14: Bas 7C 16
Lundy Cl. SS2: Sth S 6K 21
Lutea Cl. SS15: Lain 3F 15
Lych Ga. SS15: Lain 6E 14
Lychgate Ind. Est. SS6: Ray 3E 18
Lydford Rd. SS0: Wclf S 6C 32
Lylt Rd. SS8: Can I 5E 38
Lyme Rd. SS2: Sth S 4G 33
Lymington Av. SS9: Lgh S 3G 31
Lympstone Cl. SS0: Wclf S 7J 21
Lyndale Av. SS2: Sth S 2F 33
Lyndbourne Ct. SS7: Thun 6C 18
Lyndene SS7: Thun 6B 18
Lyndhurst Rd. SS4: Ashin 2J 13
(not continuous)
SS17: Corr 3F 37
Lynn Vw. Cl. SS7: Ben 7C 18
Lynstede SS14: Bas 7E 16
Lynton Rd. SS1: Sth S 7K 33
SS7: Hadl'gh 2J 29
Lynwood Grn. SS6: Ray 4C 20

M

Macaulay Av. SS16: Lan H 7C 14
Macaulay Rd. SS16: Lan H 7C 14
McCalmont Dr. SS6: Ray 4G 11
McDivitt Wlk. SS9: Lgh S 6J 21
Macdonald Av. SS0: Wclf S 3C 32
McGrail Ct. *SS8: Can I 6K 39*
(off Aalten Av.)
Macgregor Dr. SS12: Wick 6G 9
Macintyres Wlk. SS4: Ashin 5J 13
Mackenzie Cl. SS12: Wick 5G 9
Mackley Dr. SS17: Corr 2F 37
Maclaren Way SS12: Wick 6G 9
Macmurdo Cl. SS9: Lgh S 5F 21
Macmurdo Rd. SS9: Lgh S 5F 21
Madeira Av. SS9: Lgh S 3G 31
Madrid Av. SS6: Ray 5E 10
Magazine M.
SS3: Shoe 7F 35
Magazine Rd. SS3: Shoe 6E 34
Magenta Cl. CM12: Bill 4C 4
Magistrates' Court
Basildon 6J 15
Southend-on-Sea 4D 32
Magnet Ter. SS17: Stan H 3E 36
Magnolia Cl. SS8: Can I 6E 38
Magnolia La. SS15: Lain 3E 14
Magnolia Pl. SS17: Stan H 3E 36
Magnolia Rd. SS4: Ashin 5G 13
Magnolias CM11: Bill 7A 4
Magnolia Way SS4: R'fd 4E 22
Mahonia Dr. SS16: Lan H 1B 24
Main Dr. CM13: Dun 7A 14
Maine Cres. SS6: Ray 7F 11
Main Rd. CM3: Ret 4A 6
CM3: Sth F, Wdhm F 1F 7
SS5: Hawk 6E 12
SS5: Hock 6C 12
SS5: Hull 6J 7
SS7: Thun 6H 19
Main St. SS5: Hock 2C 12
Maitland Pl. SS3: Shoe 3E 34
Maitland Rd. SS12: Wick 6G 9
Malby Lodge SS0: Wclf S 5A 32
Maldon Rd. CM0: Bur C 3A 40
SS2: Sth S 4E 32
Malgraves SS13: Pit 5F 17
Malgraves Pl. SS13: Pit 5F 17
Mallard Ct. *SS1: Sth S 5G 33*
(off Windermere Rd.)
Mallard M. SS14: Bas 4A 16
Mallards SS3: Shoe 3E 34
Mallards, The SS3: Gt W 1G 35
Mallory Way CM12: Bill 6E 4
Mallow Gdns. CM12: Bill 2D 4
Malmsmead SS3: Shoe 4C 34
Maltings, The CM0: S'min 5H 41
SS11: Bat 1C 10
Maltings Ind. Est., The
CM0: S'min 5H 41
Maltings Rd. SS11: Bat 1B 10
Malting Vs. Rd. SS4: R'fd 2D 22
Malvern *SS2: Sth S 4F 33*
(off Coleman St.)
Malvern Av. SS8: Can I 5B 38
Malvern Cl. SS6: Ray 1K 19
Malvern Rd. SS5: Hock 3F 13
Malvina Cl. SS17: Horn H 6B 24
Malwood Dr. SS7: Ben 7B 18
Malwood Rd. SS7: Ben 7B 18
Malyon Ct. Cl. SS7: Thun 1H 29
Malyons SS13: Bas 4F 17
Malyons, The SS7: Thun 1H 29
Malyons Cl. SS13: Bas 4F 17
Malyons Grn. SS13: Bas 4F 17
Malyons La. SS5: Hull 1H 11
Malyons M. SS13: Bas 4F 17
Malyons Pl. SS13: Bas 4F 17
Manchester Dr. SS9: Lgh S 3F 31
(not continuous)
Mandeville Way SS7: Thun 5C 18
SS15: Bas, Lain, Lan H 6A 14
Mangapp Chase CM0: Bur C 2B 40
Mangapps Railway Mus. 2B 40
Manilla Ho. SS1: Sth S 6G 33
Manilla Rd. SS1: Sth S 6G 33
Mannering Gdns. SS0: Wclf S 2J 31
Manners Cnr. SS2: Sth S 7C 22
Manners Way SS2: Sth S 6C 22
Manning Gro. SS16: Lan H 1E 24
Manns Way SS6: Ray 6G 11
Manor Av. SS13: Pit 5G 17
Manor Cl. SS6: Ray 4K 19
Manor Ct. SS1: Sth S 6G 33
SS7: Thun 5D 18
Manor Rd. CM3: Sth F 2G 7
SS0: Wclf S 6B 32
SS5: Hock 5C 12
SS7: Thun 6C 18
SS15: Lain 5D 14
SS17: Stan H 6D 36
Manor Trad. Est. SS7: Thun 5D 18
Manor Way SS16: Pit 4H 27
SS17: Stan H 5G 37
Manorway, The
SS17: Corr, Cory, Stan H 5C 36
Mansel Cl. SS9: Lgh S 6G 21
Mansted Cl. CM13: Dun 7A 14
Mansted Gdns. SS4: Ashin 6K 13
Maple Av. SS9: Lgh S 5H 31
Maplebrook M. CM12: Bill 2D 4
Mapledene Av. SS5: Hull 1J 11
Maple Dr. SS6: Ray 4G 11
Mapleford Sweep
SS16: Vange 1B 26
Maple La. SS11: Wick 1D 8
Mapleleaf Cl. SS5: Hock 4G 13
Mapleleaf Gdns. SS12: Wick 5D 8
Maple Mead CM12: Bill 7F 5
Maples SS17: Stan H 5E 36
Maples, The SS12: Wick 6E 8
Maplesfield SS7: Hadl'gh 1K 29
Maple Sq. SS2: Sth S 3F 33
Maplestead SS14: Bas 4B 16
Maple Tree La. SS16: Lan H 7B 14
Maple Way CM0: Bur C 4B 40
SS8: Can I 5C 38
Maplewood SS8: Can I 4J 39
Maplin Cl. SS7: Thun 5C 18
Maplin Ct. *SS3: Shoe 6G 35*
(off Rampart Ter.)

54 A-Z Southend-on-Sea

Maplin Gdns. SS14: Bas 7C 16
Maplin M. SS3: Shoe 6E 34
Maplins Gdn. CM0: Bur C 4C 40
Maplin Way SS1: Sth S 5C 34
Maplin Way Nth. SS1: Sth S ..4C 34
Marcos Rd. SS8: Can I 5H 39
Marcus Av. SS1: Sth S 6B 34
Marcus Chase SS1: Sth S ..5B 34
Marcus Gdns. SS1: Sth S ..5B 34
Marden Ash SS15: Lain 6C 14
Margarite Way SS12: Wick ..3D 8
Margeth Rd. CM12: Bill 1E 14
Margeth Works CM12: Bill ..5B 4
Margraten Av. SS14: Bas ..6H 39
Marguerite Dr. SS9: Lgh S ..4H 31
Marie Cl. SS17: Fob 5J 25
Marina Av. SS6: Ray 1J 19
Marina Cl. SS2: Sth S 1C 32
Marine Activity Cen.
  Southend-on-Sea 7H 33
Marine App. SS1: Sth S 6F 33
Marine Av. SS0: Wclf S 6C 32
  SS8: Can I 6J 39
  SS9: Lgh S 4F 31
Marine Cl. SS9: Lgh S 4C 30
Marine Pde. SS1: Sth S 6F 33
  SS8: Can I 6K 39
  SS9: Lgh S 4C 30
Mariners Ct. SS3: Gt W 1J 35
Marionette Steps *SS1: Sth S* ..6G 33
  (off Kursaal Way)
Mariskals SS13: Pit 7E 16
Marjoram Cl. SS17: Stan H ..4D 36
Market Av. SS12: Wick 3E 8
Market Pavement SS14: Bas ..6J 15
Market Pl. SS1: Sth S 6E 32
Market Rd. SS12: Wick 4E 8
Market Sq. CM3: Sth F 3J 7
  SS4: R'fd 2D 22
  SS14: Bas 7J 15
Markhams SS17: Stan H 4F 37
Markhams Chase SS15: Lain ..5F 15
Markhams Ct. SS15: Lain 6F 15
Marklay Dr. CM3: Sth F 3G 7
Marks Cl. CM12: Bill 3C 4
Marks St. SS1: Sth S 6G 33
Marlborough Cl. CM12: Bill ..5D 18
Marlborough Dr. *SS16: Lan H* ..7E 14
  (off Milton Grn.)
Marlborough Pl. SS1: Sth S ..6D 32
Marlborough Rd. SS1: Sth S ..5H 33
Marlborough Wlk. SS5: Hock ..5C 12
Marlborough Way CM12: Bill ..2E 4
Marlin Cl. SS17: Hadl'gh 6A 20
Marlowe Cl. CM12: Bill 2F 5
Marlow Gdns. SS2: Sth S 1C 32
Marney Dr. SS14: Bas 7D 16
Marshall Cl. SS9: Lgh S 2C 30
Marshalls SS4: R'fd 7K 13
Marshalls Cl. SS6: Ray 2B 20
Marsh Farm Animal Adventure Pk.
  ....5J 7
Marsh Farm Country Pk. 5K 7
Marsh Farm Rd. CM3: Sth F ..6H 7
Marsh La. SS17: Fob 1K 37
Marsh Rd. CM0: Bur C 4C 40
  CM0: S'min 5J 41
  SS3: Shoe 7E 34
Marsh Vw. Ct. SS16: Vange ..2C 26
Martin Cl. CM11: Bill 6F 5
Martindale Av. SS15: Lain 2F 15
Martingale Cl. CM11: Bill 2H 5
Martingale Rd. CM11: Bill 2H 5
Martins Cl. SS17: Stan H 4D 36
Martin's Ct. SS2: Sth S 4E 32
Martins M. SS7: Ben 1C 28
Martin Wlk. SS5: Hawk 7F 13
Martyns Gro. SS0: Wclf S 3K 31
Marylands Av. SS5: Hock 4D 12
Mason Way SS3: Gt W 1F 35
Masters Cres. SS15: Lain 4D 14
Matching Grn. SS14: Bas 4B 16
Matlock Rd. SS14: Bas 5D 38
Maugham Cl. SS12: Wick 6F 9
Maurice Ct. *SS8: Can I* ..6H 39
  (off Maurice Rd.)
Maurice Rd. SS8: Can I 6H 39
Maya Cl. SS3: Shoe 5E 34
May Av. SS8: Can I 4G 39
  (not continuous)
Maydells SS13: Pit 7F 17
Maydells Ct. SS13: Pit 7F 17
Maydene CM3: Sth F 2H 5
Mayfair SS13: Pit 4G 17
Mayfair Pl. SS1: Sth S 7H 33

Mayfield Av. SS2: Sth S 1C 32
  SS5: Hull 1J 11
Mayfield Cen. CM0: Bur C 5B 40
Mayflower Cl. SS2: Sth S 6K 21
Mayflower Ct. SS8: Can I 6G 39
Mayflower Retail Pk.
  SS14: Bas 2B 16
Mayflower Rd. CM11: Bill 5F 5
Mayland Av. SS8: Can I 6D 38
Maytree Wlk. SS7: Thun 6C 18
Maze, The SS9: Lgh S 5F 21
Mead, The SS15: Lain 4D 14
Meade Cl. CM11: Bill 2H 5
Meade Rd. CM11: Bill 2H 5
Meadgate SS13: Bas 4G 17
Meadow Cl. SS7: Thun 6H 19
Meadow Ct. CM11: Bill 5G 5
  SS8: Can I 2D 38
  SS11: Wick 3G 9
Meadow Dr. SS1: Sth S 5J 33
  SS16: Lan H 5D 24
Meadowland Rd. SS11: Wick ..5J 9
Meadow M. CM3: Sth F 2F 7
Meadow Ri. CM11: Bill 5G 5
  SS5: Hull 1J 11
  SS7: Hadl'gh 3A 30
Meadowside SS6: Ray 2K 19
  SS7: Ben 2B 28
Meadow Vw. SS16: Lan H 1A 24
Meadow Vw. Wlk. SS8: Can I ..4C 38
Meadow Way CM0: Bur C 3B 40
  SS5: Hock 6E 12
  SS12: Wick 1H 17
Meadow Way, The CM11: Bill ..5G 5
Meads, The SS16: Vange 2E 26
Meadway SS0: Wclf S 5K 31
  SS6: Ray 3B 20
  SS7: Thun 5C 18
  SS8: Can I 6G 39
Meakins Cl. SS9: Lgh S 5H 21
Mecca Bingo
  Southend-on-Sea 4F 33
Medoc Cl. SS13: Pit 4G 17
Medway *CM0: Bur C* 4B 40
  (off Maple Way)
Medway Cres. SS9: Lgh S 4D 30
Meesons Mead SS4: R'fd 1B 22
Meggison Way SS7: Ben 2C 28
Melcombe Rd. SS7: Ben 2C 28
Mellow Mead SS15: Lain 4D 14
Mellow Purgess SS15: Lain 6E 14
Mellow Purgess Cl.
  SS15: Lain 6E 14
Mellow Purgess End
  SS15: Lain 6E 14
  (off Victoria Rd.)
Melville Ct. *SS1: Sth S* 7H 33
Melville Dr. SS12: Wick 7F 9
Melville Heath CM3: Sth F 4J 7
Memorial App. SS11: Wick 2G 9
Mendip Cl. SS6: Ray 1A 20
  SS11: Wick 4G 9
Mendip Cres. SS0: Wclf S 7J 21
Mendip Rd. SS0: Wclf S 1J 31
Mentmore SS16: Lan H 1D 24
Menzies Av. SS15: Lain 6B 14
Meppel Av. SS8: Can I 2E 38
Mercer Av. SS3: Gt W 1G 35
Mercer Rd. CM11: Bill 2H 5
Merchant St. CM3: Sth F 3J 7
Mercury Cl. SS11: Wick 3H 9
Meredene SS14: Bas 7D 16
Mereworth Rd. CM3: Sth F 5G 7
Meriadoc Dr. CM3: Sth F 4H 7
Meridian Point SS2: Sth S 5G 33
Merilies Cl. SS0: Wclf S 2K 31
Merilies Gdns. SS0: Wclf S ..2K 31
Merlin Ct. SS8: Can I 4F 39
Merlin Way SS11: Runw 2F 9
Merricks La. SS16: Vange 3C 26
Merrigold Cl. SS7: Thun 7H 19
Merrivale SS7: Ben 3C 28
Merriwigs La. SS16: Pit 3C 26
Merrydown SS15: Lain 5C 14
Merryfield SS9: Lgh S 1G 31
Merryfield App. SS9: Lgh S ..2G 31
Merryfields Av. SS5: Hock 4D 12
Merrylands Chase CM13: Dun ..5A 14
Mersea Cres. SS12: Wick 5H 9
Merton Pl. CM3: Sth F 4K 7
Merton Rd. SS5: Hock 3A 12
  SS7: Ben 1C 28
Mess Rd. SS3: Shoe 7F 35

Meteor Rd. SS0: Wclf S 5B 32
Methersgate SS14: Bas 5A 16
Metz Av. SS8: Can I 4E 38
Mews, The SS5: Hock 5C 12
Meyel Av. SS8: Can I 3G 39
Meynell Av. SS8: Can I 6G 39
MFA Bowl & Rendezvous Casino
  Southend-on-Sea 6G 33
Michael's Cotts. SS3: Shoe ..6D 34
Mid Colne SS16: Vange 1B 26
Middle Cloister CM11: Bill 5F 5
Middle Crockerford
  SS16: Vange 1C 26
Middle Dr. SS17: Fob 4K 25
Middle Mead SS4: R'fd 2D 22
  SS11: Wick 3H 9
Middlesburg SS8: Can I 3C 38
Middlesex Av.
  SS9: Lgh S, Wclf S 2H 31
Middleton Row CM3: Sth F ..4J 7
Midhurst Av. SS0: Wclf S 1B 32
Midsummer Mdw. SS3: Shoe ..3E 34
Milbanke Cl. SS3: Shoe 3E 34
Milbourn Ct. SS4: R'fd 2D 22
Mildmayes SS16: Lan H 1E 24
Mildmay Ind. Est. CM0: Bur C ..5C 40
Mildmay Rd. CM0: Bur C 5D 40
Miles Gray Rd. SS14: Bas 3H 15
Milestone Cl. SS5: Hawk 7F 13
Military Cl. SS3: Shoe 4E 34
Millars Cl. CM3: Sth F 2J 7
Mill Cotts. SS11: Bat 1B 10
Mill Fld. Cl. SS6: Ray 1A 20
Millfield CM0: Bur C 6C 40
  CM11: Bill 6F 5
Millfields Cvn. Site
  CM0: Bur C 6B 40
Mill Grange CM0: Bur C 3C 40
Mill Grn. CM0: Bur C 3C 40
Mill Grn. Ct. SS13: Pit 5F 17
Mill Grn. Rd. SS13: Pit 5F 17
Millhead Way SS4: R'fd 3F 23
Mill Hill SS7: Ben 5E 28
Mill Hill Dr. CM12: Bill 2F 5
Mill La. SS4: R'fd 3D 22
  SS17: Fob 1J 37
  SS17: Horn H 4A 36
Mill La. Nth. SS17: Fob 6K 25
Mill La. Sth. SS17: Fob 6A 26
Mill Meadows Nature Reserve ..5F 5
Mill Rd. CM0: Bur C 3C 40
  CM11: Bill 7B 4
Millview Ct. SS4: R'fd 3D 22
Millview Mdws. SS4: R'fd 3D 22
Milner Pl. CM12: Bill 2D 4
Milton Av. SS0: Wclf S 6C 32
  SS16: Lan H 1B 24
Milton Cl. SS2: Sth S 4E 32
  SS6: Ray 2C 20
  (not continuous)
Milton Ct. SS0: Wclf S 6C 32
Milton Grn. SS16: Lan H 7E 14
Milton Hall Cl. SS3: Gt W 1G 35
Milton Pl. SS1: Sth S 6D 32
Milton Rd. SS0: Wclf S 6C 32
  SS17: Corr, Stan H 7F 37
Milton St. SS2: Sth S 4E 32
Miltsin Av. SS8: Can I 3G 39
Mimosa Cl. SS16: Lan H 1B 24
Minster Cl. SS6: Ray 3C 20
Minster Rd. SS15: Lain 6E 14
Minton Hgts. SS4: Ashin 5J 13
Miramar Av. SS8: Can I 5C 38
Mirror Steps *SS1: Sth S* 6G 33
  (off Kursaal Way)
Mistley End SS16: Vange 7A 16
Mistley Path SS16: Vange 7A 16
Mistley Side SS16: Vange 7A 16
  (not continuous)
Mitchells Av. SS8: Can I 4H 39
Mitchells Wlk. SS8: Can I 4H 39
Mitchell Way CM3: Sth F 2H 7
Moat Edge Gdns. CM12: Bill ..3E 4
Moat End SS1: Sth S 3B 34
Moat Fld. SS14: Bas 4A 16
Moat Ho. Lodge *SS14: Bas* ..4A 16
  (off Church Rd.)
Moat Ri. SS6: Ray 3K 19
Molineaux Cl. CM12: Bill 4E 4
Mollands SS16: Vange 1D 26
Mollys Dr. SS16: Lan H 2C 24
Monarch Cl. SS11: Wick 4H 9

Monastery Rd. SS15: Lain 6E 14
Monksford Dr. SS5: Hull 2H 11
Monks Haven SS17: Stan H ..4E 36
Monkside SS14: Bas 5B 16
Monmouth M. SS16: Lan H ..7B 14
Monoux Cl. CM11: Bill 6H 5
Mons Av. CM11: Bill 5H 5
Montague Av. SS9: Lgh S 3D 30
Montague Bldgs. SS1: Sth S ..5F 33
Montague Cl. SS0: Wclf S 5B 32
Montague Pl. SS14: Bas 5C 38
Montague Side SS14: Bas 3D 16
Montague St. SS14: Bas 3D 16
Montague Way CM12: Bill 3E 4
Montefiore Av. SS6: Ray 3G 11
Montfort Av. SS17: Corr 3G 37
Montgomery Cl. SS3: Shoe ..3E 34
Montgomery Dr. SS14: Bas ..5C 16
Montpelier Cl. CM12: Bill 2E 4
Montsale SS13: Pit 4G 17
Moons Cl. SS4: Ashin 4K 13
Moorcroft SS4: Ashin 5K 13
Moorcroft Av. SS7: Hadl'gh ..6A 20
Moore Cl. CM11: Bill 2H 5
Moores Av. SS17: Fob 4A 26
Moor Pk. Cl. SS9: Lgh S 7E 20
Moor Pk. Gdns. SS9: Lgh S ..7E 20
Mopsies Rd. SS14: Bas 6C 16
Moreland Av. SS7: Thun 6C 18
Moreland Cl. SS7: Thun 6C 18
Moreland Rd. SS11: Wick 1E 8
Moretons SS13: Pit 6E 16
Moretons Ct. SS13: Pit 6E 16
Moretons M. SS13: Pit 6E 16
Moretons Pl. SS13: Pit 6E 16
Morley Hill SS17: Stan H 1F 37
Morley Link
  SS17: Corr, Stan H 2F 37
Mornington Av. SS4: R'fd 2E 22
Mornington Cres.
  SS7: Hadl'gh 2B 30
  SS8: Can I 4G 39
Mornington Ho. SS0: Wclf S ..6A 32
Mornington Rd. SS8: Can I 3F 39
Morrells SS16: Bas 1H 25
Morrin's Chase
  SS3: Gt W, Shoe 1K 35
Morris Av. CM11: Bill 6H 5
Morris Cl. SS15: Lain 5D 14
Mortar Cl. SS3: Shoe 4D 34
Mortimer Rd. SS6: Ray 6H 11
Moseley St. SS2: Sth S 4H 33
Moss Cl. SS16: Vange 2C 26
Moss Dr. SS16: Vange 2C 26
Mosses La.
  CM3: Sth F, Wdhm F 1E 6
Motehill SS16: Lan H 1E 24
Mount, The CM11: Bill 4J 5
  SS17: Stan H 4F 37
Mountain Ash Av. SS9: Lgh S ..6D 20
Mountain Ash Cl. SS9: Lgh S ..6D 20
Mount Av. SS0: Wclf S 4J 31
  SS5: Hock 5D 12
  SS6: Ray 1J 19
Mountbatten Dr. SS3: Shoe ..3E 34
Mt. Bovers La. SS5: Hawk 1G 21
Mount Cl. SS6: Ray 2J 19
  SS11: Wick 3G 9
Mount Cres. SS5: Hock 5D 12
  SS7: Ben 1E 28
Mountdale Gdns. SS9: Lgh S ..1G 31
Mountfield Cl. SS17: Stan H ..4E 36
Mountfields SS13: Pit 1F 27
Mt. Liell Cl. SS9: Lgh S 6A 32
Mountnessing SS7: Hadl'gh ..3K 29
Mountnessing Rd. CM12: Bill ..1B 4
Mt. Pleasant Rd. CM3: Sth F ..3H 7
Mount Rd. SS7: Ben 2F 29
  (not continuous)
  SS11: Wick 3G 9
Mount Vw. CM11: Bill 5J 5
Mountview Ct. SS16: Vange ..2C 26
Mount Way SS11: Wick 3G 9
Mount Zion SS7: Hadl'gh 4K 29
Movie Starr
  Canvey Island 6G 39
Muir Pl. SS12: Wick 6F 9
Muirway SS7: Thun 5B 18
Mulberry Gdns. SS16: Lan H ..7D 14
Mulberry Rd. SS8: Can I 5A 38
Mulberrys, The SS2: Sth S 2E 32
Mullions, The CM12: Bill 4D 4
Mundells Dr. SS15: Lain 5G 15
Munro Cl. SS12: Wick 6G 9
Munsons All. CM0: S'min 5G 41
Munsons Ct. CM0: S'min 5G 41

Munsterburg Rd.—Oyster Cl.

Munsterburg Rd. SS8: Can I 3H 39
Munster Ct. CM12: Bill 2D 4
Murray Way SS12: Wick 6F 9
Murrels La. SS5: Hock 4A 12
Musket Gro. SS9: Lgh S 5D 20
Mustang Cl. SS4: R'fd 6K 13
Mynchens SS15: Lain 6G 15

N

Namur Rd. SS8: Can I 4G 39
Nansen Av. SS4: Ashin 5K 13
Napier Av. SS1: Sth S 5D 32
Napier Cl. SS14: Bas 6B 16
Napier Ct. W. *SS1: Sth S* 5D 32 *(off Gordon Pl.)*
Napier Cres. SS12: Wick 6G 9
Napier Gdns. SS7: Thun 6J 19
Napier Rd. SS6: Ray 1B 20
Nave, The SS15: Lain 5F 15
Navestock Cl. SS6: Ray 1G 19
Navestock Gdns. SS1: Sth S 4K 33
Nayland Cl. SS12: Wick 4G 9
Nayland Ho. SS2: Sth S 7C 22
Nazareth Ho. SS2: Sth S 5D 32
Nazeing, The SS14: Bas 6C 16
Needham Cl. CM11: Bill 4F 5
Neil Armstrong Way SS9: Lgh S 5J 21
Nelson Cl. SS6: Ray 7K 11
Nelson Ct. CM0: Bur C 6D 40
Nelson Dr. SS9: Lgh S 4H 31
Nelson Gdns. SS6: Ray 7K 11
Nelson M. SS1: Sth S 6E 32
Nelson Pl. CM3: Sth F 4J 7
Nelson Rd. SS4: Ashin 5K 13
SS6: Ray 1B 20
SS9: Lgh S 3J 31
SS14: Bas 6C 16
Nelson St. SS1: Sth S 6E 32
Nesbit Cl. SS12: Wick 6E 8
Ness Rd. SS3: Shoe 5D 34
Nestuda Ho. SS9: Lgh S 5D 20
Nestuda Way SS2: Sth S 6K 21
Netherfield SS7: Thun 1G 29
Nether Mayne SS16: Bas, Vange 7J 15
Nether Priors SS14: Bas 6A 16
Nevada Rd. SS8: Can I 3G 39
NEVENDON 1F 17
Nevendon Bushes Nature Reserve 4E 16
Nevendon Grange SS12: Wick 5E 8
Nevendon M. SS13: Bas 2E 16
Nevendon Rd. SS12: Wick 1E 16 (not continuous)
SS13: Bas 2E 16
Nevendon Trad. Est. SS13: Bas 3F 17
Nevern Cl. SS6: Ray 4B 20
Nevern Rd. SS6: Ray 4A 20
Neville Shaw SS14: Bas 6K 15
Nevyll Ct. SS1: Sth S 4B 34
New Av. SS16: Lan H 1C 24
New Barge Pier Rd. SS3: Shoe 7E 34
Newberry Side SS15: Lain 6E 14
New Century Rd. SS15: Lain 6C 14
New Cotts. SS13: Pit 7H 17
Newell Av. SS3: Shoe 4G 35
New England Cres. SS3: Gt W 2J 35
New Farm Cotts. SS3: Shoe 4D 34
New Garrison Rd. SS3: Shoe 6E 34
Newhall SS4: Ashin 5J 13
New Hall Rd. SS5: Hock 2G 13
Newhouse Av. SS12: Wick 4B 8
Newington Av. SS2: Sth S 3H 33
Newington Cl. SS2: Sth S 3K 33
Newington Gdns. SS2: Sth S 3J 33
Newlands Cl. CM12: Bill 2F 5
Newlands End SS15: Lain 4D 14
Newlands Rd. CM12: Bill 3F 5
SS8: Can I 3H 39 (not continuous)
SS12: Wick 7F 9
New Lodge 6C 4
New Moor Cl. CM0: S'min 5H 41
New Moor Cres. CM0: S'min 5H 41
New Pk. Rd. SS5: Hock 3G 13
SS7: Ben 7C 18
Newport Ct. SS6: Ray 7F 11
New Rd. CM0: Bur C 5D 40
CM12: L Bur 2C 14
SS3: Gt W 1H 35
SS7: Hadl'gh 2K 29
SS8: Can I 5C 38
SS9: Can I, Lgh S 5F 31
New Sq. SS5: Hock 2C 12
Newstead Rd. SS3: Gt W 1H 35
Newsum Gdns. SS6: Ray 1G 19
NEW THUNDERSLEY 5D 18
Newton Cl. SS17: Corr 2G 37
Newton Hall Gdns. SS4: Ashin 5K 13
Newton Pk. Rd. SS7: Thun 5H 19
Newton Rd. SS14: Bas 4D 16
New Waverley Rd. SS15: Bas 3G 15
Nicholl Rd. SS15: Lain 5D 14
Nicholson Cres. SS7: Thun 2H 29
Nicholson Gro. SS12: Wick 6G 9
Nicholson Ho. SS1: Sth S 5F 33
Nicholson Rd. SS7: Thun 2H 29
Nightingale Cl. SS2: Sth S 6C 22
SS6: Ray 1H 19
Nightingale Gro. SS14: Bas 5C 16
Nightingale Rd. SS8: Can I 5G 39
Nightingales SS16: Lan H 7B 14
Niton Ct. SS17: Stan H 7C 36
Niven Cl. SS12: Wick 6G 9
NOAK BRIDGE 3G 15
Noak Bridge Nature Reserve 3H 15
NOAK HILL 1E 14
Noak Hill Cl. CM12: Bill 1D 14
Noak Hill Golf Course 1E 14
Noak Hill Rd. CM12: Bill 1E 14, 7F 5
SS15: Bas, Lain 1E 14
Nobel Sq. SS13: Bas 2G 17
NOBLESGREEN 5G 21
Nobles Grn. Cl. SS9: Lgh S 5G 21
Nobles Grn. Rd. SS9: Lgh S 5G 21
Nordland Rd. SS8: Can I 4H 39
Noredale SS3: Shoe 7D 34
Nore Rd. SS9: Lgh S 4E 20
Nore Vw. SS16: Lan H 2B 24
Norfolk Av. SS9: Lgh S 2H 31
Norfolk Cl. SS8: Can I 3E 38
SS15: Lain 6C 14
Norfolk Ct. SS4: Ashin 6K 13
Norfolk Way SS8: Can I 3D 38
Norman Cres. SS6: Ray 6J 11
Normandy Av. CM0: Bur C 5D 40
Norman Harris Ho. SS1: Sth S 6F 33
Norman Pl. *SS9: Lgh S* 5G 31 *(off Church Hill)*
Normans Rd. SS8: Can I 4H 39
Norman Ter. *SS9: Lgh S* 5G 31 *(off Leigh Hill)*
Norsey Cl. CM11: Bill 4F 5
Norsey Dr. CM11: Bill 4G 5
Norsey Rd. CM11: Bill 5F 5
Norsey Vw. Dr. CM12: Bill 1F 5
Norsey Wood Information Cen. 3H 5
Norsey Wood Nature Reserve 4H 5
Northampton Gro. SS16: Lan H 1B 24
North Av. SS2: Sth S 4F 33
SS8: Can I 4D 38
NORTH BENFLEET 4K 17
Nth. Benfleet Hall Rd. SS12: Nth B 3K 17
North Colne SS16: Vange 1B 26
North Cres. SS2: Sth S 7A 22
SS12: Wick 4F 9
North Crockerford SS16: Vange 1C 26
North Dr. CM13: Hut 4A 4
NORTHEND 4H 41
North End CM0: S'min 4H 41
Northern Av. SS7: Ben 7C 18
Northfalls Rd. SS8: Can I 5K 39 (not continuous)
Northfield Cl. CM11: Bill 5G 5
Northfield Ho. SS2: Sth S 4D 32
Northfields Cres. SS3: Gt W 1H 35
North Gunnels SS14: Bas 6K 15
North Hill SS17: Horn H 7B 24
Northlands App. SS16: Bas 4E 24
Northlands Cl. SS17: Stan H 2E 36
Northlands Pavement SS13: Pit 7F 17
Northlands Pl. SS13: Bas 4E 16
North Rd. CM11: C Hill 6A 8
SS0: Wclf S 3C 32
Nth. Sea Crossing SS17: Stan H 7H 37
NORTH SHOEBURY 3D 34
Nth. Shoebury Rd. SS3: Shoe 3D 34
North St. CM0: S'min 5G 41
SS3: Gt W 1H 35
SS4: R'fd 2D 22
SS9: Lgh S 5G 31
Northumberland Av. SS1: Sth S 6G 33
SS15: Lain 7E 14
Northumberland Cres. SS1: Sth S 6H 33
Northview Dr. SS0: Wclf S 4A 32
Northville Dr. SS0: Wclf S 1A 32
Nth. Weald Cl. SS11: Wick 5K 9
Northwick Rd. SS8: Can I 4A 38
Norton Av. SS8: Can I 5J 39
Norton Cl. SS17: Corr 3G 37
Norwich Av. SS2: Sth S 2G 33
Norwich Cl. SS2: Sth S 3G 33
Norwich Cres. SS6: Ray 6G 11
Norwood Dr. SS7: Ben 4E 28
Norwood End SS14: Bas 5B 16
Nottage Cl. SS17: Corr 3F 37
Nottingham Way SS16: Lan H 7B 14
Nursery Cl. SS6: Ray 3K 19
Nursery Dr. SS5: Hawk 1H 21
Nursery Gdns. SS15: Lain 4E 14
Nursery Rd. SS17: Stan H 4E 36
Nutcombe Cres. SS4: R'fd 7K 13
Nuthatch Cl. CM11: Bill 7G 5

O

Oak Av. CM11: C Hill 1A 16
SS11: Raw, Wick 4A 10
Oak Chase SS12: Wick 4C 8
Oak Ct. SS7: Hadl'gh 3A 30
Oak Cres. SS11: Wick 1D 8
Oakdene Rd. SS13: Pit 4G 17
Oaken Grange Dr. SS2: Sth S 7C 22
Oakfield Cl. SS7: Ben 2C 28
Oakfield Rd. SS7: Ben 2C 28
Oak Grn. CM11: Bill 6H 5
Oakham Cl. SS16: Lan H 7B 14
Oakham Ct. SS9: Lgh S 3G 31
Oakhurst Cl. SS12: Wick 5E 8
Oakhurst Dr. SS12: Wick 5D 8
Oakhurst Rd. SS2: Sth S 3E 32
SS6: Ray 4B 20
Oaklands SS8: Can I 4J 39
Oaklands Farm Ind. Est. CM4: Stock 1K 5
Oaklands M. SS4: R'fd 7J 13
Oak La. CM11: C Hill 1A 16
Oakleigh Av. SS1: Sth S 5H 33
SS5: Hull 1J 11
Oakleigh Pk. Dr. SS9: Lgh S 4G 31
Oakleighs SS7: Ben 1C 28
Oakley Av. SS6: Ray 1F 19
Oakley Dr. CM12: Bill 2D 4
Oak Lodge SS5: Hock 6E 12
Oak Rd. CM11: C Hill 7A 8 (1K 15)
SS4: R'fd 2C 22
SS8: Can I 5G 39
Oak Rd. Nth. SS7: Hadl'gh 3A 30
Oak Rd. Sth. SS7: Hadl'gh 3A 30
Oaks, The CM11: Bill 7A 4
SS7: Thun 1H 29
Oak Tree Gdns. SS0: Wclf S 1K 31
Oakview Cl. SS9: Lgh S 2G 31
Oak Wlk. SS5: Hock 4E 12
SS7: Thun 4B 18 (not continuous)
SS9: Lgh S 1F 31
Oakway St. SS5: Hock 1C 12
Oakwood Av. SS9: Lgh S 1G 31
Oakwood Cl. SS7: Ben 7B 18
Oakwood Ct. SS9: Lgh S 7G 21
Oakwood Dr. CM12: Bill 2G 5
Oakwood Gro. SS13: Pit 6F 17
Oakwood Rd. SS6: Ray 7G 11
SS17: Corr 3H 37
Oasis Ct. SS2: Sth S 3E 32
Oast Ct. SS4: R'fd 2D 22
Oast Way SS4: R'fd 2D 22
Oban Ct. SS11: Wick 6J 9
Oban Rd. SS2: Sth S 4G 33
Odeon Cinema Southend-on-Sea 5E 32
Odessa Rd. SS8: Can I 5G 39
O'Donaghue Ho's. SS17: Stan H 5E 36
Ogilvie Ct. SS12: Wick 6G 9
Old Church Hill SS16: Lan H 4A 24
Old Church Rd. CM13: Bill, Mount 1A 4
SS13: B Gif 7K 17
Old Farm Ct. CM12: Bill 3E 4
Old Fortune Cotts. SS15: Lain 3F 15
Old Hall Ct. SS3: Gt W 1G 35
Old Hill Av. SS16: Lan H 5D 24
Old House, The Rochford 3D 22
Old Jenkins Cl. SS17: Stan H 6B 36
Old Leigh Rd. SS9: Lgh S, Wclf S 4J 31
Old London Rd. SS11: Raw 5B 10
Old Mkt. Retail Pk. SS13: Pit 7F 17
Old Mead SS2: Sth S 5J 21
Old Nevendon Rd. SS12: Wick 1F 17
Old Rectory Ct. SS2: Sth S 4J 33
Old School Mdw. SS3: Gt W 1E 34
Old Ship La. SS4: R'fd 2D 22
Old Southend Rd. SS1: Sth S 6F 33
Old Wickford Rd. CM3: Sth F 2F 7
Oldwyk SS16: Vange 1C 26
Olive Av. SS9: Lgh S 3C 30
Olivers Cres. SS3: Gt W 1G 35
Olivia Dr. SS9: Lgh S 3H 31
Olympic Bus. Cen. SS14: Bas 2D 16
One Tree Hill SS16: Bas, Vange 3H 25
SS17: Fob, Vange 3H 25
Optical Ct. SS2: Sth S 3E 32
Orange Rd. SS8: Can I 4H 39
Orchard, The SS12: Wick 4D 8
Orchard Av. CM11: Ram 1A 8
CM12: Bill 2G 5
SS5: Hock 4E 12
SS6: Ray 4J 19
Orchard Cl. CM0: S'min 5G 41
SS3: Gt W 1H 35
SS5: Hock 4F 13
Orchard Ct. CM12: Bill 3D 4
Orchard Gro. SS9: Lgh S 6H 21
Orchard Mead SS9: Lgh S 7G 21
Orchard Rd. CM0: Bur C 6D 40
CM0: S'min 5G 41
SS7: Thun 5B 18
Orchards SS8: Can I 3J 39
Orchard Side SS9: Lgh S 6H 21
Orchard Vw. CM13: Dun 7A 14
Orchid Pl. CM3: Sth F 2H 7
SS15: Lain 7F 15
Orchill Dr. SS7: Hadl'gh 1A 30
Orion Ct. SS14: Bas 3D 16
Orkney Gdns. SS12: Wick 6H 9
Orlando Dr. SS13: Bas 3G 17
Ormesby Chine CM3: Sth F 5G 7
Ormonde Av. SS4: R'fd 1C 22
SS7: Hadl'gh 3C 30
Ormonde Gdns. SS9: Lgh S 3C 30
Ormond Ho. *SS4: R'fd* 2D 22 *(off Roche Cl.)*
Ormsby Rd. SS8: Can I 6B 38
Ormo Rd. SS8: Can I 5K 39
Orsett Av. SS9: Lgh S 7E 20
Orsett End SS14: Bas 5A 16
Orsett Rd. SS17: Horn H 4A 36
Orwell Ct. SS11: Wick 6K 9
Orwell Way CM0: Bur C 4B 40
Osborne Av. SS5: Hock 5C 12
Osborne Rd. SS0: Wclf S 4C 32
SS13: B Gif 4J 17
SS16: Vange 7A 16
Osbourne Ho. SS0: Wclf S 4A 32
Osier Dr. SS15: Lain 3E 14
Osprey Cl. SS3: Shoe 3E 34
Ospreys, The *SS9: Lgh S* 4H 31 *(off Leigh Rd.)*
OSTEND 3A 40
Osterley Dr. SS16: Lan H 7B 14
Osterley Pl. CM3: Sth F 5H 7
Ouida Rd. SS8: Can I 5H 39
Oulton Av. SS8: Can I 3D 38
Outing Cl. SS1: Sth S 6G 33
Outwood Comn. Rd. CM11: Bill 3J 5
Outwood Farm Cl. CM11: Bill 5J 5
Outwood Farm Rd. CM11: Bill 5J 5
Overcliff SS0: Wclf S 6B 32
Overmead Dr. CM3: Sth F 2J 7
Overton Cl. SS7: Thun 6C 18
Overton Dr. SS7: Thun 6C 18
Overton Rd. SS7: Thun 6B 18
Overton Way SS7: Thun 6B 18
Ovington Gdns. CM12: Bill 2E 4
Oxcroft Ct. SS15: Lain 6D 14
Oxford Cl. SS16: Lan H 7B 14
Oxford Rd. SS4: R'fd 7K 13
SS8: Can I 4G 39
SS17: Stan H 6B 36
Oxley Gdns. SS17: Stan H 2D 36
Oxwich Cl. SS17: Corr 3G 37
Oyster Cl. CM0: Bur C 6D 40

56 A-Z Southend-on-Sea

Prittlewell Station (Rail)—Rookyards

Prittlewell Station (Rail) ... 2E 32
Prittlewell St. SS2: Sth S ... 4E 32
Professional Pl. SS11: Wick ... 6J 9
Progress Bus. Pk. SS9: Lgh S ... 5E 20
Progress Rd. SS9: Lgh S ... 6E 20
Promenade, The CM0: Bur C ... 6B 40
SS1: Sth S ... 7B 34
SS3: Shoe ... 7B 34
SS5: Hull ... 7H 7
Prospect Av. SS17: Stan H ... 6B 36
Prospect Cl. SS1: Sth S ... 6G 33
Prospect Stadium, The ... 6K 39
Protea Way SS8: Can I ... 4F 39
Prout Ind. Est. SS8: Can I ... 5K 39
Providence CM0: Bur C ... 6D 40
Prower Cl. CM11: Bill ... 6F 5
Puck La. SS16: Bas ... 7A 16
Puckleside SS16: Lan H ... 1E 24
Puffin Cl. SS12: Wick ... 6H 9
Puffin Pl. SS3: Shoe ... 3E 34
Pugh Pl. SS17: Stan H ... 3D 36
Pullman Ct. SS11: Wick ... 3F 9
Pulpits Cl. SS5: Hock ... 4F 13
Pump Mead Cl. CM0: S'min ... 5G 41
Pump St. SS17: Horn H ... 5A 36
Purcell Cl. SS15: Lain ... 4F 15
SS17: Stan H ... 4C 36
Purcell Way SS17: Stan H ... 4C 36
Purdeys Ind. Est. SS4: R'fd ... 4E 22
Purdeys Way SS4: R'fd ... 4E 22
PureGym
Billericay ... **4E 4**
Thorpe Bay ... **2A 34**
Purleigh Cl. SS13: Bas ... 3G 17
Purleigh Rd. SS6: Ray ... 1H 19
Purley Way SS0: Wclf S ... 7A 22

Q

Quantock SS1: Sth S ... 5E 32
Quarter Ga. CM3: Sth F ... 5J 7
Quatro Pk. SS14: Bas ... 2D 16
Quay, The CM0: Bur C ... 6D 40
Quebec Av. SS1: Sth S ... 5F 33
Quebec Gdns. CM3: Sth F ... 4H 7
Queen Anne's Cl. SS0: Wclf S ... 1A 32
Queen Anne's Dr. SS0: Wclf S ... 1A 32
Queen Anne's M. SS0: Wclf S ... 1A 32
Queen Ann's Gro. SS5: Hull ... 3H 11
Queenborough Rd.
CM0: S'min ... 5G 41
Queen Elizabeth II Sq.
CM3: Sth F ... 3J 7
Queen Elizabeth Chase
SS4: R'fd ... 5D 22
Queen Elizabeth Dr.
SS17: Corr ... 2F 37
Queens Av. SS5: Hull ... 6J 7
SS9: Lgh S ... 4G 31
Queen's Ct. SS9: Lgh S ... 5H 31
Queens Ct. CM0: Bur C ... 6C 40
SS9: Lgh S ... 4G 31
Queens Ga. M. CM12: Bill ... 2D 4
Queensland Av. SS4: R'fd ... 5D 22
Queens Lodge SS7: Hadl'gh ... 2J 29
Queens Mall *SS1: Sth S ... 6E 32*
(within The Royals Shop. Cen.)
Queensmere SS7: Thun ... 1H 29
QUEEN'S PARK ... 2F 5
Queens Pk. Av. CM12: Bill ... 3E 4
Queen's Pk. Country Pk. ... **1F 5**
Queens Pk. Ct. CM12: Bill ... 2D 4
Queen's Rd. SS1: Sth S ... 5D 32
SS7: Ben ... 3D 28
Queens Rd. CM0: Bur C ... 5C 40
SS6: Ray ... 3K 19
SS9: Lgh S ... 5H 31
SS15: Lain ... 3E 14
Queen St. CM0: S'min ... 5F 41
Queensway SS1: Sth S ... 5F 33
SS2: Sth S ... 5D 32
Queenswood Rd.
SS17: Stan H ... 7B 36
Quendon Rd. SS14: Bas ... 4C 16
Quest End SS6: Ray ... 6H 11
Quilters Cl. SS14: Bas ... 4B 16
Quilters Dr. CM12: Bill ... 7E 4
Quilters Straight SS14: Bas ... 4B 16
Quorn Gdns. SS9: Lgh S ... 4C 30

R

Rachael Clarke Cl.
SS17: Corr ... 3E 36
Rackenford SS3: Shoe ... 4D 34
Radford Bus. Cen. CM12: Bill ... 4D 4
Radford Ct. CM12: Bill ... 4F 5
Radford Cres. CM12: Bill ... 4E 4
Radford Ho. CM12: Bill ... 4F 5
Radford Way CM12: Bill ... 4D 4
Radnor Rd. SS4: Ashin ... 2J 13
Radstocks CM12: Bill ... 4F 5
Radwinter Av. SS12: Wick ... 4F 9
Railway App. SS15: Lain ... 5C 14
(not continuous)
Railway Ter. SS2: Sth S ... 2E 32
Rainbow Av. SS8: Can I ... 4G 39
Rainbow La. SS17: Stan H ... 5F 37
Rainbow Rd. SS8: Can I ... 4G 39
Raleigh Dr. SS15: Lain ... 7F 15
Ramblers Way CM0: Bur C ... 6E 40
Ramparts, The SS6: Ray ... 2B 20
Rampart St. SS3: Shoe ... 6F 35
Rampart Ter. SS3: Shoe ... 6G 35
Ramsay Dr. SS16: Vange ... 2C 26
RAMSDEN BELLHOUSE ... 3A 8
Ramsden Ct. SS12: Wick ... 4F 9
Ramsden Pk. Rd.
CM11: Ram ... 1A 8
Ramsden Vw. Rd. SS12: Wick ... 5B 8
Ramsey Chase SS12: Wick ... 5H 9
Ramsey Ct. SS0: Wclf S ... 2K 31
Ramuz Dr. SS0: Wclf S ... 4B 32
Randolph Cl. SS9: Lgh S ... 2G 31
Randway SS6: Ray ... 3K 19
Rantree Fold SS16: Bas ... 1H 25
Raphael Dr. SS3: Shoe ... 4F 35
Raphaels SS15: Lain ... 7G 15
Rat La. SS6: Ray ... 4J 19
Ratsborough Chase
CM0: S'min ... 7F 41
Rattwick Dr. SS8: Can I ... 5K 39
Raven Cl. CM12: Bill ... 3D 4
Raven Cres. CM12: Bill ... 3D 4
Ravendale Way SS3: Shoe ... 2D 34
Raven Dr. SS7: Ben ... 3B 28
Raven La. CM12: Bill ... 3D 4
Ravens Ct. SS1: Sth S ... 6D 32
Ravenscourt Dr. SS16: Vange ... 7C 16
Ravensdale SS16: Bas, Vange ... 1K 25
Ravensfield SS14: Bas ... 6D 16
Ravensfield Ct. SS14: Bas ... 6D 16
Ravenswood Chase SS4: R'fd ... 5D 22
RAWRETH ... 4C 10
Rawreth Gdns. SS11: Raw ... 2C 10
Rawreth Ind. Est. SS6: Ray ... 6E 10
Rawreth La. SS6: Ray ... 4D 10
SS11: Raw, Ray ... 4D 10
RAWRETH SHOT ... 4A 10
Ray Cl. SS8: Can I ... 6E 38
SS9: Lgh S ... 4D 30
RAYLEIGH ... 2K 19
Rayleigh Av. SS0: Wclf S ... 4C 32
SS9: Lgh S ... 4D 20
Rayleigh Cl. SS9: Lgh S, Ray ... 4D 20
Rayleigh Downs Rd.
SS6: Ray ... 5C 20
Rayleigh Dr. SS9: Lgh S ... 2F 31
Rayleigh Golf Course, The ... **3H 11**
Rayleigh Indoor Karting Stadium
... **4J 19**
Rayleigh Leisure Cen. ... **6F 11**
Rayleigh Mount ... **2J 19**
Rayleigh Rd. CM13: Hut ... 5A 4
SS7: Hadl'gh, Thun ... 5H 19
SS9: Lgh S, Sth S ... 5D 20
SS17: Stan H ... 6B 36
Rayleigh Station (Rail) ... 1J 19
Rayleigh Tower Mill ... **1K 19**
Rayment Av. SS8: Can I ... 5H 39
Raymonds Cl. CM3: Sth F ... 3G 7
Raymonds Dr. SS7: Thun ... 6F 19
Rayne Path SS13: Pit ... 7E 16
Rayside SS14: Bas ... 6A 16
(not continuous)
Ray Wlk. SS9: Lgh S ... 4D 30
Read Cl. SS5: Hawk ... 7G 13
Reading Cl. SS16: Lan H ... 7B 14
Rebels La. SS3: Gt W ... 1A 34 (2J 33)
Recreation Av. SS9: Lgh S ... 3H 31
SS16: Lan H ... 2C 24
SS17: Corr ... 2J 37
Rectory Av. SS4: Ashin ... 4H 13
Rectory Cl. SS7: Hadl'gh ... 2A 30
Rectory Cotts. SS16: Vange ... 3A 26
Rectory Ct. SS13: Pit ... 5G 17
Rectory Gdns. SS13: Pit ... 6G 17
Rectory Gth. SS6: Ray ... 1K 19
Rectory Gro. SS9: Lgh S ... 5F 31
SS11: Wick ... 4H 9
Rectory La. SS11: Bat ... 4C 6
Rectory Pk. Dr. SS13: Pit ... 7F 17
Rectory Rd. CM12: L Bur ... 1B 14
SS4: R'fd ... 7J 13
SS5: Hawk ... 1H 21
SS7: Hadl'gh ... 2A 30
SS13: Pit ... 7G 17
(not continuous)
SS17: Stan H ... 6C 36
Rectory Ter. SS5: Hawk ... 7G 13
SS17: Stan H ... 6C 36
Redcliff Dr. SS9: Lgh S ... 5H 31
Redgate Cl. SS11: Wick ... 3J 9
Redgrave Rd. SS16: Vange ... 1C 26
Redhills Rd. CM3: Sth F ... 2J 7
Redinge, The CM11: Bill ... 6B 4
Redlie Cl. SS17: Stan H ... 3D 36
Redshank Cl. SS14: Bas ... 4A 16
Redshank Cres. CM3: Sth F ... 1H 7
Redstock Rd. SS2: Sth S ... 3E 32
Redwing Dr. CM11: Bill ... 7G 5
Redwood Dr. SS15: Lain ... 3F 15
Redwoods, The SS8: Can I ... 5C 38
Reed Pond Wlk. SS16: Lan H ... 1D 24
Reeds Cl. SS15: Lain ... 3C 14
Reeds Way SS12: Wick ... 3E 8
Reeves Cl. SS16: Lan H ... 1B 24
Reeves Way CM3: Sth F ... 3J 7
Regan Cl. SS17: Stan H ... 3E 36
Regatta Ct. SS9: Lgh S ... 5H 31
Regency Cl. SS4: R'fd ... 2C 22
SS11: Runw ... 1F 9
Regency Ct. SS5: Hock ... 5E 12
Regency Grn. SS2: Sth S ... 2D 32
Regent Cl. SS6: Ray ... 7F 11
Regent Ct. SS15: Lain ... 4G 15
Regent Dr. CM12: Bill ... 2D 4
Regents Cl. CM0: S'min ... 5G 41
Regents Ct. CM0: Bur C ... 6C 40
Rembrandt Cl. SS3: Shoe ... 4G 35
SS8: Can I ... 5E 38
Remembrance Av.
CM0: Bur C ... 6C 40
Renacres SS16: Bas ... 1H 25
Renown Shop. Cen., The
SS3: Shoe ... 4F 35
Repton Cl. SS13: Bas ... 3E 16
Repton Ct. SS13: Bas ... 3E 16
Repton Gro. SS2: Sth S ... 5J 21
Retort Cl. SS1: Sth S ... 7H 33
Retreat Rd. SS0: Wclf S ... 6C 32
SS5: Hock ... 5E 12
RETTENDON ... 5A 6
Rettendon Cl. SS6: Ray ... 1G 19
Rettendon Gdns. SS11: Wick ... 2G 9
Rettendon Vw. SS11: Wick ... 3H 9
Reynolds Gdns. SS4: Ashin ... 5J 13
Reynolds Ga. CM3: Sth F ... 4J 7
Rhoda Rd. SS7: Ben ... 1D 28
(not continuous)
Rhoda Rd. Nth. SS7: Thun ... 7E 18
Rhum M. SS12: Wick ... 6J 9
Richmond Av. SS0: Wclf S ... 5C 32
SS1: Sth S ... 6E 32
(off High St.)
SS3: Shoe ... 5D 34
SS7: Ben ... 3C 28
Richmond Dr. SS0: Wclf S ... 1A 32
SS6: Ray ... 4K 19
Richmond Rd. SS11: Wick ... 1E 8
Richmond St. SS2: Sth S ... 4H 33
Ricketts Dr. CM12: Bill ... 4D 4
Rickling SS16: Vange ... 1D 26
Ridgemount SS7: Ben ... 1E 28
Ridgeway CM12: Bill ... 7E 4
SS5: Hull ... 6J 7
SS6: Ray ... 3J 19
Ridgeway, The SS0: Wclf S ... 5J 31
Ridgeway Gdns. SS0: Wclf S ... 5K 31
Ridings, The SS4: R'fd ... 3D 22
SS8: Can I ... 3E 38
Ridley Rd. SS13: Bas ... 3G 17
Riffams Ct. SS13: Bas ... 4G 17
Riffams Dr. SS13: Bas ... 4G 17
Ringwood Dr. SS9: Lgh S ... 5D 20
Rio Cinema
Burnham-on-Crouch ... **6D 40**
Rippleside SS14: Bas ... 7D 16
Rise Pk. SS15: Lain ... 6H 15
Rising, The CM11: Bill ... 6H 5
Rivendell Va. CM3: Sth F ... 4G 7
Rivenhall SS6: Thun ... 4H 19
SS11: Wick ... 5J 9
Riverdale SS9: Lgh S ... 5F 21
Riverside Ct. *SS11: Wick ... 3F 9*
(off Lwr. Southend Rd.)
Riverside Ho. *SS11: Wick ... 3F 9*
(off Lwr. Southend Rd.)
Riverside Ind. Est. SS4: R'fd ... 3D 22
Riverside Rd. CM0: Bur C ... 6D 40
Riverside Wlk. SS12: Wick ... 3D 8
Riverstone SS0: Wclf S ... 5A 32
Rivertons SS16: Vange ... 1D 26
River Vw. SS12: Wick ... 4E 8
Riverview SS5: Hull ... 6J 7
SS8: Can I ... 3K 39
SS16: Vange ... 1E 26
River Vw. Cl. SS15: Lain ... 3E 14
Riverview Ct. SS16: Vange ... 1C 26
Riverview Gdns. SS5: Hull ... 7G 7
River Vw. Rd. SS7: Ben ... 3D 28
Riverview Wlk. SS5: Hull ... 7H 7
Riviera Dr. SS1: Sth S ... 5G 33
Roach Av. SS6: Ray ... 3J 19
Roach Va. SS9: Lgh S ... 5H 21
Roach Vw. Bus. Pk. SS4: R'fd ... 3F 23
Robert Cl. CM12: Bill ... 5D 4
Robert Leonard Ind. Est.
SS2: Sth S ... 5A 22
Robert Leonard Ind. Pk.
SS2: Sth S ... 7D 22
Robertson Dr. SS12: Wick ... 6G 9
Roberts Rd. SS15: Lain ... 5D 14
Robert Way SS11: Wick ... 5H 9
Robin Cl. CM12: Bill ... 1G 5
Robinia Cl. SS15: Lain ... 3F 15
Robinsons Cl. CM0: S'min ... 6F 41
Robins Path SS7: Thun ... 1H 29
Roche Av. SS4: R'fd ... 2C 22
Roche Cl. SS4: R'fd ... 2D 22
Rochefort Dr. SS4: R'fd ... 4D 22
Rocheforte Ho. SS4: R'fd ... 2D 22
Rochehall Way SS4: R'fd ... 4E 22
Rochester Dr. SS0: Wclf S ... 1A 32
Rochester M. SS0: Wclf S ... 1A 32
Rochester Way SS14: Bas ... 5D 16
Rocheway SS4: R'fd ... 2D 22
ROCHFORD ... 2D 22
Rochford Av. SS0: Wclf S ... 4C 32
Rochford Bus. Pk. SS4: Sth S ... 5K 21
Rochford Cl. SS11: Wick ... 5H 9
Rochford Gdn. Way SS4: R'fd ... 1C 22
Rochford Hall Cl. SS4: R'fd ... 3D 22
Rochford Hall Cotts.
SS4: R'fd ... 3B 22
ROCHFORD HOSPITAL ... **2C 22**
Rochford Hundred Golf Course
... **3C 22**
Rochford Rd. SS2: Sth S ... 1B 32
SS8: Can I ... 5H 39
Rochford Station (Rail) ... 3C 22
Rockall SS2: Sth S ... 5J 21
Rockleigh Av. SS9: Lgh S ... 4J 31
Rodbridge Dr. SS1: Sth S ... 5K 33
Roding Cl. SS3: Gt W ... 1H 35
Roding Leigh CM3: Sth F ... 3J 7
Rodings, The SS9: Lgh S ... 5F 21
Rodings Av. SS17: Stan H ... 3D 36
Roding Way SS12: Wick ... 5G 9
Roedean Cl. SS2: Sth S ... 4K 33
Roedean Cres. SS15: Lain ... 3C 14
Roedean Gdns. SS2: Sth S ... 3K 33
Roggel Rd. SS8: Can I ... 6H 39
Rohan Ct. CM3: Sth F ... 4H 7
Rokells SS14: Bas ... 5J 15
Rokescroft SS13: Pit ... 7E 16
Roland La. SS8: Can I ... 4F 39
Rolla City ... **4E 22**
Romagne Cl. SS17: Horn H ... 4A 36
Romainville Way SS8: Can I ... 5A 38
Roman Ct. SS11: Wick ... 6J 9
Romans Farm Chase
CM0: Bur C ... 3D 40
Roman Way CM0: Bur C ... 3C 40
CM12: Bill ... 7E 4
Romany Steps *SS1: Sth S ... 6G 33*
(off Beresford Rd.)
Romney Ho. SS4: R'fd ... 2D 22
Romney Rd. CM12: Bill ... 6D 4
Romsey Cl. SS5: Hock ... 5D 12
SS7: Ben ... 7B 18
SS17: Stan H ... 6B 36
Romsey Cres. SS7: Ben ... 7B 18
Romsey Dr. SS7: Ben ... 7B 18
Romsey Rd. SS7: Ben ... 7A 18
Romsey Way SS7: Ben ... 7B 18
Ronald Dr. SS6: Ray ... 7E 10
Ronald Hill Gro. SS9: Lgh S ... 4F 31
Ronald Pk. Av. SS0: Wclf S ... 4A 32
Roodegate SS14: Bas ... 6J 15
Rookery Cl. SS6: Ray ... 2J 19
SS17: Stan H ... 6B 36
Rookery Hill ... **4H 37**
Rookery Hill SS17: Corr ... 4H 37
Rookery Mead CM3: Sth F ... 2H 7
Rookyards SS16: Vange ... 7C 16

58 A-Z Southend-on-Sea

Roosevel Av.—Seaview Av.

Roosevel Av. SS8: Can I 4E 38
Roosevelt Rd. SS15: Lain 6C 14
Roots Hall 3C 32
Roots Hall Av. SS2: Sth S 3D 32
Roots Hall Dr. SS2: Sth S 3C 32
Rosary Gdns. SS0: Wclf S 1K 31
Rosbach Rd. SS8: Can I 5H 39
Rosberg Rd. SS8: Can I 5J 39
Roscommon Way SS8: Can I 4A 38
Rose Acre SS14: Bas 6D 16
Rose & Crown M.
CM0: S'min 5G 41
Rosebay Av. CM12: Bill 2D 4
Roseberry Av. SS7: Thun 6C 18
SS16: Lan H 1D 24
Roseberry Ct. SS7: Thun 5C 18
Roseberry Wlk. SS7: Thun 5C 18
Rose Cl. SS12: Wick 6G 9
Rose Ct. SS17: Corr 3H 37
Rosecroft Cl. SS16: Lan H 1C 24
Rose Dr. CM0: S'min 6G 41
Roselaine SS14: Bas 5K 15
Rose La. CM12: Bill 5E 4
Rosemary M. SS17: Stan H 5D 36
Rosemead SS7: Thun 5C 18
Roserna Rd. SS8: Can I 5H 39
Rose Rd. SS8: Can I 5E 38
Rose St. SS7: Thun 7H 19
Rose Valley Cres.
SS17: Stan H 3E 36
Rose Way SS4: R'fd 4E 22
Rosewood La. SS3: Shoe 5F 35
Rosilian Dr. SS5: Hock 2C 12
Rosshill Ind. Pk. SS2: Sth S 1E 32
Rossiter Rd. SS3: Shoe 4H 35
Rosslyn Cl. SS5: Hock 4E 12
Rosslyn Rd. CM12: Bill 5D 4
SS5: Hock 4E 12
Ross Way SS16: Lan H 2D 24
Rothwell Cl. SS9: Lgh S 6E 20
Roundacre SS15: Lain 6J 15
Round Hill Rd. SS7: Ben 3G 29
Rowallen La. CM12: Bill 1D 4
Rowan Cl. SS6: Ray 5F 11
Rowans, The CM11: Bill 7H 5
SS9: Lgh S 6D 20
Rowans Way SS11: Wick 3G 9
Rowan Wlk. SS9: Lgh S 6F 21
Rowenhall SS15: Lain 6B 14
Rowhedge Cl. SS13: Bas 2G 17
Rowlands, The SS7: Ben 2E 28
Roxborough Gdns.
SS16: Vange 7B 16
Roxwell Cres. SS12: Wick 5G 9
Royal Artillery Way
SS2: Sth S 2H 33
Royal Burnham Yacht Club 7D 40
Royal Cl. SS4: Ashin 6K 13
Royal Ct. *SS2: Sth S 4E 32*
(off Guildford Rd.)
SS9: Lgh S 4D 20
Royal M. SS1: Sth S 6E 32
Royal Oak Chase SS15: Lain 4G 15
Royal Oak Dr. SS11: Wick 3J 9
Royal Pavilion, The *6E 32*
(on Southend Pier)
Royals Shop. Cen., The
SS1: Sth S 6E 32
Royal Ter. SS1: Sth S 6E 32
Roydon Bri. SS14: Bas 4B 16
Royer Cl. SS5: Hawk 7G 13
Royston Av. SS2: Sth S 2E 32
SS15: Lain 3F 15
Rubens Cl. SS3: Shoe 4G 35
Rubicon Av. SS11: Wick 3H 9
Ruby Ct. SS9: Lgh S 7G 21
Ruffles Cl. SS6: Ray 1A 20
Rumbullion Dr. CM12: Bill 4D 4
Rundells Wlk. SS14: Bas 5C 16
Rundels, The SS7: Thun 7G 19
Rundels Cotts. *SS7: Thun 6G 19*
(off The Rundels)
Runnymede Chase SS7: Thun 1G 29
Runnymede Ct. SS17: Stan H 6C 36
Runnymede Rd. SS8: Can I 5F 39
SS17: Stan H 6C 36
Runnymede Swimming Pool &
Sports Hall 7G 19
RUNWELL 2G 9
Runwell Chase SS11: Runw 1J 9
Runwell Gdns. SS11: Runw 1F 9
Runwell Rd.
SS11: Runw, Wick 3F 9 (7A 6)
Runwell Ter. SS1: Sth S 6D 32
Runwood Rd. SS8: Can I 5A 38
Rupert Jarvis Ct. SS5: Hock 5D 12
Rupert Rd. CM0: S'min 5F 41
Rushbottom La. SS7: Thun 5B 18
SS12: Nth B 3B 18
Rush Cl. SS7: Thun 6B 18
Rushdene Rd. CM12: Bill 6D 4
Rushes La. CM0: Ashel 1K 41
Rushley SS13: Bas, Pit 4H 17
Rushley Cl. SS3: Gt W 1G 35
Ruskin Av. SS2: Sth S 3F 33
Ruskin Dene CM12: Bill 4E 4
Ruskin Path SS12: Wick 6F 9
Ruskin Rd. SS17: Stan H 6C 36
Ruskoi Rd. SS8: Can I 3D 38
Russell Cl. SS15: Lain 6D 14
Russell Ct. SS11: Wick 4H 9
Russell Gdns. SS11: Wick 4G 9
Russell Gro. SS4: R'fd 2E 22
Russel Sq. SS15: Lain 6B 14
Russet Cl. SS17: Stan H 4D 36
Russetts SS16: Lan H 7C 14
Russetts, The SS4: Ashin 6K 13
Russet Way CM0: Bur C 4D 40
SS5: Hock 3E 12
Rutherford Cl. CM12: Bill 2E 4
SS9: Lgh S 6E 20
Ruthven Cl. SS12: Wick 6F 9
Rutland Av. SS1: Sth S 5J 33
Rutland Cl. SS15: Lain 6C 14
Rutland Dr. SS6: Ray 4F 11
Rutland Gdns. SS4: Ashin 6J 13
Rydal Cl. SS5: Hull 7H 7
SS6: Ray 2A 20
Ryde, The SS9: Lgh S 7D 20
Ryde Cl. SS9: Lgh S 7D 20
Ryde Dr. SS17: Stan H 7C 36
Ryder Way SS13: Bas 2H 17
Ryedene SS16: Vange 2C 26
Ryedene Cl. SS16: Vange 2C 26
Ryedene Pl. SS16: Vange 2C 26
Rye Mead SS16: Lan H 1E 24
Rylands Rd. SS2: Sth S 3G 33

S

Sable Ct. SS15: Lain 5B 14
Sable Way SS15: Lain 5B 14
Sackville Rd. SS2: Sth S 4J 33
Sadlers SS7: Thun 6B 18
Sadlers Cl. CM11: Bill 2H 5
Saffory Cl. SS9: Lgh S 5E 20
Saffron Cl. SS17: Horn H 4A 36
Saffron Ct. *SS11: Wick 1E 8*
(off Saffron Dr.)
SS15: Lain 6B 14
Saffron Dr. SS11: Wick 1E 8
SS14: Bas 5B 16
Saffron Wlk. CM11: Bill 5F 5
Sage M. SS17: Stan H 4E 36
Sains SS15: Lain 5F 15
St Agnes Dr. SS8: Can I 5B 38
St Agnes Rd. CM12: Bill 1E 14
St Andrews Cl. SS3: Shoe 6E 34
SS8: Can I 4B 38
St Andrews Dr. CM11: Bill 4F 5
St Andrews La. SS15: Lain 5E 14
St Andrew's Rd. SS3: Shoe 6C 34
St Andrews Rd. SS4: R'fd 2C 22
St Andrews Way SS17: Stan H 7B 36
St Annes Rd. SS8: Can I 5H 39
St Anns Cl. SS15: Lain 5E 14
St Ann's Rd. SS2: Sth S 4E 32
St Augustine's Av. SS1: Sth S 6B 34
St Benet's Rd. SS2: Sth S 2D 32
St Catherines Cl. SS11: Wick 3H 9
St Chads Cl. SS15: Lain 5E 14
St Charles Dr. SS11: Wick 4G 9
St Christophers Cl. SS8: Can I 4B 38
St Clare Mdw. SS4: R'fd 1D 22
St Clements Av. SS9: Lgh S 3G 31
St Clement's Cl. SS5: Hawk 7G 13
SS7: Ben 7C 18
St Clements Ct. SS9: Lgh S 5F 31
St Clements Ct. E. SS9: Lgh S 5F 31
St Clement's Cres. SS7: Ben 7D 18
St Clements Dr. SS9: Lgh S 2G 31
St Clement's Rd. SS7: Ben 1C 28
St Cleres Cres. SS11: Wick 4H 9
St Clere's Hall Golf Course 7B 36
St David's Ct. SS16: Vange 2C 26
St Davids Dr. SS9: Lgh S 2C 30
St David's Rd. SS16: Lan H 1D 24
St Davids Ter. SS9: Lgh S 2C 30
St Davids Wlk. SS8: Can I 4B 38
St David's Way SS11: Wick 4G 9
St Edith's Ct. CM12: Bill 6E 4
SS9: Lgh S 5H 31
St Edith's La. CM12: Bill 6E 4
St Edmund's Cl. SS2: Sth S 2G 33
St Francis Ct. *SS2: Sth S 4G 33*
(off Stornoway Rd.)
St Gabriels Ct. SS13: Pit 7F 17
St George's Dr. SS0: Wclf S 2C 32
St George's La. SS3: Shoe 6F 35
St George's Pk. Av.
SS0: Wclf S 4K 31
St George's Wlk. SS7: Thun 6B 18
SS8: Can I 4B 38
St Guiberts Rd. SS8: Can I 3C 38
St Helen's Rd. SS0: Wclf S 5C 32
St Helens Wlk. CM12: Bill 3D 4
St James Av. SS1: Sth S 6B 34
St James Av. E.
SS17: Stan H 4E 36
St James Av. W. SS17: Stan H 4E 36
St James Cl. SS0: Wclf S 2J 31
SS8: Can I 4B 38
St James Ct. SS8: Can I 7F 39
St James Gdns. SS0: Wclf S 2J 31
St James M. CM12: Bill 5E 4
St James Rd. SS16: Vange 7B 16
(not continuous)
St James's Wlk. *SS5: Hock 5C 12*
(off Belvedere Av.)
St Johns Cl. SS3: Gt W 1H 35
SS15: Lain 5E 14
St John's Ct. SS0: Wclf S 6D 32
St Johns Cres. SS8: Can I 4B 38
St Johns Dr. SS6: Ray 7C 10
St John's M. SS17: Corr 3F 37
St John's Rd. CM11: Bill 4F 5
SS0: Wclf S 5C 32
SS3: Gt W 1H 35
SS7: Hadl'gh 2J 29
St John's Way SS17: Corr 3F 37
St Katherines Ct. SS8: Can I 5C 38
St Katherine's Heritage Cen. 5B 38
St Lawrence Ct. SS9: Lgh S 6G 21
St Lawrence Gdns.
SS9: Lgh S 6G 21
St Leonard's Rd. SS1: Sth S 6F 33
St Lukes Cl. SS8: Can I 4B 38
SS15: Lain 5E 14
ST LUKE'S HOSPICE 1J 25
St Lukes Pl. SS4: R'fd 2C 22
St Luke's Rd. SS2: Sth S 2G 33
St Margaret's Av.
SS17: Stan H 7C 36
St Marks Fld. SS4: R'fd 1D 22
St Mark's Rd. SS7: Hadl'gh 2J 29
St Marks Rd. SS8: Can I 4B 38
St Martins Bell Tower 6J 15
St Martin's Cl. SS6: Ray 4J 19
SS7: Thun 5B 18
St Martins Sq. SS14: Bas 6J 15
St Mary's Av. CM12: Bill 5E 4
St Mary's Cl. SS3: Shoe 3D 34
SS7: Ben 4D 28
St Mary's Ct. SS2: Sth S 3C 32
St Mary's Cres. SS13: Pit 6G 17
St Mary's Dr. SS7: Ben 4D 28
St Mary's Path SS13: Pit 5G 17
St Mary's Rd. CM0: Bur C 4C 40
SS2: Sth S 3D 32
SS7: Ben 5D 28
St Marys Rd. SS12: Wick 6D 8
St Michaels Av. SS13: Pit 1F 27
St Michael's Rd.
SS7: Hadl'gh, Ray 6B 20
St Michaels Rd. SS8: Can I 4B 38
St Nicholas La. SS15: Lain 5E 14
St Omer Cl. SS12: Wick 5G 9
St Pauls Ct. *SS0: Wclf S 5C 32*
(off Salisbury Av.)
St Pauls Gdns. CM12: Bill 3E 4
St Paul's Rd. SS8: Can I 4B 38
St Peter's Ct. SS0: Wclf S 1A 32
St Peters Fld. CM0: Bur C 3B 40
St Peter's Pavement
SS14: Bas 3D 16
St Peters Rd. SS5: Hock 4B 12
SS8: Can I 4B 38
St Peter's Ter. SS12: Wick 4E 8
St Peters Wlk. CM12: Bill 3D 4
St Teresa's Cl. SS14: Bas 7D 16
St Vincents M. SS0: Wclf S 5C 32
St Vincents Rd. SS0: Wclf S 6C 32
Sairard Cl. SS9: Lgh S 5F 21
Sairard Gdns. SS9: Lgh S 5F 21
Salcott Cres. SS12: Wick 4F 9
Salcott M. *SS12: Wick 5H 9*
(off Twinstead)
Salem Wlk. SS6: Ray 7F 11
Salesbury Dr. CM11: Bill 5H 5
Saling Grn. SS15: Bas 2H 15
Salisbury Av. SS0: Wclf S 4C 32
SS17: Stan H 6D 36
Salisbury Cl. SS6: Ray 6G 11
Salisbury Ct. SS9: Lgh S 4F 31
SS16: Lan H 7E 14
(off Milton Grn.)
Salisbury M. SS0: Wclf S 4C 32
Salisbury Rd. SS9: Lgh S 3E 30
Saltcoats CM3: Sth F 2H 7
Saltings, The SS7: Hadl'gh 2K 29
Samson Ho. SS15: Lain 3D 14
Samuel Rd. SS16: Lan H 1D 24
SAMUEL'S CORNER 1K 35
Samuels Dr. SS1: Sth S 4B 34
Sanctuary Gdns.
SS17: Stan H 5E 36
Sanctuary Rd. SS9: Lgh S 2C 30
Sandbanks SS7: Hadl'gh 3K 29
Sanderlings SS7: Ben 3C 28
Sanderson Ct. SS7: Ben 7C 18
Sanders Rd. SS8: Can I 2E 38
Sandhill Rd. SS9: Lgh S 4E 20
Sandhurst SS8: Can I 5A 38
Sandhurst Cl. SS9: Lgh S 1H 31
Sandhurst Cres. SS9: Lgh S 1H 31
Sand Island Cen. CM0: Bur C 5B 40
Sandleigh Rd. SS9: Lgh S 4J 31
Sandon Cl. SS4: R'fd 1B 22
SS14: Bas 7D 16
Sandon Ct. SS14: Bas 7C 16
Sandon Rd. SS14: Bas, Pit 7D 16
Sandown Av. SS0: Wclf S 3K 31
Sandown Cl. SS11: Wick 4J 9
Sandown Rd. SS7: Thun 5H 19
SS11: Wick 4J 9
Sandpiper Cl. SS3: Shoe 4E 34
Sandpiper La. SS14: Bas 4A 16
Sandpipers *SS3: Shoe 6G 35*
(off Rampart Ter.)
Sandpit La. CM0: Bur C 5D 40
Sandpit Rd. SS3: Shoe 4H 35
Sandringham Av. SS5: Hock 5C 12
Sandringham Cl.
SS17: Stan H 4E 36
Sandringham Ct.
SS7: Hadl'gh 3A 30
Sandringham Rd. SS1: Sth S 5H 33
SS15: Lain 4G 15
Sangster Ct. SS6: Ray 2A 20
San Remo Pde. SS0: Wclf S 6C 32
San Remo Rd. SS8: Can I 5H 39
Sans Souci *SS9: Lgh S 5F 31*
(off Leigh Pk. Rd.)
Sark Gro. SS12: Wick 6H 9
Satanita Rd. SS0: Wclf S 5A 32
Savannah Hgts. SS9: Lgh S 4J 31
Savoy Cl. SS16: Lan H 7C 14
Saxon Cl. SS6: Ray 6J 11
SS11: Runw 2G 9
Saxon Ct. SS7: Ben 7C 18
Saxon Gdns. SS3: Shoe 5C 34
Saxon Pl. SS4: R'fd 2D 22
Saxonville SS7: Ben 1B 28
Saxon Way SS7: Ben 3C 28
Sayers SS7: Thun 6G 19
Scaldhurst SS13: Pit 4G 17
Scarborough Dr. SS9: Lgh S 3G 31
Scarletts SS14: Bas 4A 16
Scholars Cres. SS15: Lain 4C 14
Scholars Wlk. CM3: Sth F 2J 7
School Av. SS15: Lain 4D 14
School La. SS7: Ben 5D 28
SS12: Nth B 2A 18
School Path SS15: Lain 4D 14
School Rd. CM12: Bill 7E 4
School Way SS9: Lgh S 2H 31
Scimitar Pk. Ind. Est.
SS13: Bas 2H 17
Scott Dr. SS12: Wick 6F 9
Scott Ho. SS9: Lgh S 5J 21
Scotts Wlk. SS6: Ray 2C 20
Scratton Rd. SS1: Sth S 6D 32
SS17: Stan H 5D 36
Scrub La. SS7: Hadl'gh 2A 30
Scrub Ri. CM12: Bill 7D 4
Seabrink SS9: Lgh S 5H 31
Sea-End Cvn. Site CM0: Bur C 6E 40
Seaforth Av. SS2: Sth S 3G 33
Seaforth Gro. SS2: Sth S 3H 33
Seaforth Rd. SS0: Wclf S 6B 32
Sea Life Adventure
Southend-on-Sea 7G 33
Seamore Av. SS7: Thun 6C 18
Seamore Cl. SS7: Thun 6B 18
Seamore Wlk. SS7: Thun 5C 18
Sea Reach SS9: Lgh S 5G 31
Seaview Av. SS16: Vange 2B 26

A-Z Southend-on-Sea 59

Thorndon Pk. Dr.—Wall Rd.

Thorndon Pk. Dr. SS9: Lgh S 7D 20
Thorney Bay Cvn. Pk.
SS8: Can I 7E 38
Thorney Bay Rd. SS8: Can I 5D 38
Thornford Gdns. SS2: Sth S 7D 22
Thornhill SS9: Lgh S 1G 31
Thornton Way SS15: Lain 6C 14
Thornwood Ct. SS9: Lgh S 6F 21
Thorolds SS16: Vange 2C 26
THORPE BAY 4B 34
Thorpe Bay Gdns. SS1: Sth S 6A 34
Thorpe Bay Sailing Club 6B 34
Thorpe Bay Station (Rail) 4B 34
Thorpe Cl. SS5: Hawk 7F 13
SS12: Wick 5H 9
Thorpedene Av. SS5: Hull 1J 11
Thorpedene Gdns. SS3: Shoe 5D 34
Thorpe Esplanade SS1: Sth S 7K 33
Thorpe Gdns. SS5: Hawk 7F 13
THORPE GREEN 5F 35
Thorpe Green M. SS3: Shoe 5F 35
Thorpe Hall Av. SS1: Sth S 3A 34
Thorpe Hall Cl. SS1: Sth S 4A 34
Thorpe Hall Golf Course 5A 34
Thorpe Rd. SS5: Hawk 7F 13
Thorp Leas SS8: Can I 6F 39
Thorrington Cross SS14: Bas 6A 16
Thors Oak SS17: Stan H 5E 36
Threshelford SS16: Bas 1H 25
Throwley Cl. SS13: Pit 7G 17
THUNDERSLEY 6F 19
Thundersley Chu. Rd.
SS7: Thun 7D 18
Thundersley Gro. SS7: Thun 7F 19
Thundersley Oaks Nature Pk. 5E 18
Thundersley Pk. Rd.
SS7: Ben 3D 28
Thurlow Dr. SS1: Sth S 5K 33
Thurlstone SS7: Thun 7J 19
Thurston Av. SS2: Sth S 4J 33
Thynne Rd. CM11: Bill 5G 5
Tickfield Av. SS2: Sth S 3D 32
Tideway *SS1: Sth S* *7H 33*
(off Eastern Esplanade)
Tidworth Av. SS11: Runw 1G 9
Tighfield Wlk. CM3: Sth F 5H 7
Tilburg Rd. SS8: Can I 4E 38
(not continuous)
Tillingham Grn. SS15: Lain 6C 14
Tillingham Rd. CM0: Ashel 2K 41
CM0: S'min 4H 41
Tillingham Way SS6: Ray 1G 19
Tilney Turn SS16: Vange 1C 26
(not continuous)
Timberlog Cl. SS14: Bas 6C 16
Timberlog La. SS14: Bas 6C 16
Timberlog Pl.
SS16: Bas, Vange 7C 16
Timbermans Vw.
SS16: Vange 1D 26
Time Sq. SS14: Bas 7J 15
Tinker's La. SS4: R'fd 4D 22
Tinkler Side SS14: Bas 6K 15
Tintern Av. SS0: Wclf S 4A 32
Tintern M. SS0: Wclf S 4A 32
Tippersfield SS7: Ben 1E 28
Tiptree Cl. SS9: Lgh S 1H 31
Tiptree Gro. SS12: Wick 4F 9
Tiree Chase SS12: Wick 6H 9
Tithe, The SS12: Wick 5D 8
Toledo Cl. SS1: Sth S 5F 33
Toledo Rd. SS1: Sth S 5F 33
Tollesbury Cl. SS12: Wick 5G 9
Tollgate SS7: Thun 6J 19
Tomkins Cl. SS17: Stan H 4C 36
Tonbridge Rd. SS5: Hock 3F 13
Tongres Rd. SS8: Can I 4E 38
Took Dr. CM3: Sth F 4G 7
Toppesfield Av. SS12: Wick 6E 8
Torney Cl. SS16: Lan H 1B 24
Torquay Cl. SS6: Ray 6H 11
Torquay Dr. SS9: Lgh S 4G 31
Torrington SS3: Shoe 4D 34
Torsi Rd. SS8: Can I 5H 39
Totman Cl. SS6: Ray 4K 19
Totman Cres. SS6: Ray 4K 19
Toucan Cl. SS3: Shoe 3E 34
Toucan Way SS16: Bas 2J 25
Tourist Info. Cen.
Southend-on-Sea 6E 32
Tower Av. SS15: Lain 5E 14
Tower Ct. SS0: Wclf S 6C 32
Tower Ct. M. SS0: Wclf S 6C 32
Towerfield Cl. SS3: Shoe 5E 34
Towerfield Rd. SS3: Shoe 5E 34
Towerfield Rd. Ind. Est.
SS3: Shoe 5E 34
Tower Pk. SS5: Hull 7J 7
Tower Side SS5: Hull 6J 7
Townfield Rd. SS4: R'fd 2D 22
Townfields SS2: Sth S 3E 32
Townfield Wlk. SS3: Gt W 1E 34
Towngate Theatre 6J 15
Town Sq. SS14: Bas 6J 15
Trafalgar Rd. SS3: Shoe 5D 34
Trafalgar Way CM12: Bill 2F 5
Trafford Ho. SS9: Lgh S 3H 31
SS16: Bas 7J 15
Travers Way SS13: Pit 6E 16
Treebeard Copse CM3: Sth F 4F 7
Treecot Dr. SS9: Lgh S 1H 31
Treelawn Dr. SS9: Lgh S 1H 31
Treelawn Gdns. SS9: Lgh S 1H 31
Trenders Av. SS6: Ray 5F 11
Trenham Av. SS13: Pit 5G 17
Trent Cl. CM0: Bur C 4B 40
SS12: Wick 5F 9
Tresco Way SS12: Wick 6H 9
Treviria Av. SS8: Can I 4G 39
Trevor Cl. CM12: Bill 7D 4
Triangle, The *SS16: Lan H* *1D 24*
(off High Rd.)
Trianon Ct. SS13: Pit 6G 17
Trimley Cl. SS14: Bas 5A 16
Trindehay SS15: Lain 7G 15
Trinder Way SS12: Wick 5D 8
Trinity Av. SS0: Wclf S 6C 32
Trinity Cl. CM11: Bill 7A 4
SS6: Ray 3A 20
SS15: Lain 6E 14
Trinity Rd. CM11: Bill 7A 4
SS2: Sth S 4G 33
SS6: Ray 3A 20
Trinity Row CM3: Sth F 3J 7
Trinity Sq. CM3: Sth F 3J 7
Trinity Wood Rd. SS5: Hock 3G 13
Tripat Cl. SS17: Fob 2K 37
Triton Way SS7: Thun 6G 19
Tropical Wings Zoo 2E 6
Troubridge Cl. CM3: Sth F 3K 7
Truman Cl. SS15: Lain 6C 14
Trumpeter Ct. CM12: Bill 4D 4
Trunnions, The SS4: R'fd 3D 22
Truro Cres. SS6: Ray 6G 11
Tudor Av. SS17: Stan H 3E 36
Tudor Chambers *SS13: Pit* *7F 17*
(off Station La.)
Tudor Cl. SS6: Ray 2B 20
SS7: Thun 7F 19
SS9: Lgh S 5E 20
Tudor Ct. SS15: Bas 2H 15
Tudor Gdns. SS3: Shoe 5D 34
SS9: Lgh S 2F 31
Tudor Mans. SS13: Pit 7F 17
Tudor M. SS2: Sth S 3D 32
SS9: Lgh S 4E 20
Tudor Rd. SS0: Wclf S 3C 32
SS8: Can I 5B 38
SS9: Lgh S 5E 20
Tudor Wlk. SS12: Wick 4C 8
Tudor Way SS5: Hawk 7F 13
SS12: Wick 4C 8
Tunbridge Av. SS2: Sth S 3E 32
Tunbridge Rd. SS2: Sth S 3D 32
Tunstall Cl. SS13: Pit 7G 17
Turner Cl. SS3: Shoe 4F 35
SS15: Lain 7F 15
Turold Rd. SS17: Stan H 3E 36
Turpins SS14: Bas 5A 16
Tutors Way CM3: Sth F 3J 7
Twain Ter. SS12: Wick 6E 8
Twin Oaks Wlk. SS6: Ray 7F 11
Twinstead SS12: Wick 5G 9
Two Tree Island Nature Reserve
2K 39
Twyford Av. SS3: Gt W 1G 35
Twyzel Rd. SS8: Can I 4G 39
TYE COMMON 7D 4
Tye Comn. Rd.
CM12: Bill, L Bur 7C 4
Tyefields SS13: Pit 5G 17
Tyelands CM12: Bill 7D 4
Tyler Av. SS15: Lain 6E 14
Tylers Av. CM12: Bill 2F 5
SS1: Sth S 6E 32
Tylers Ride CM3: Sth F 3J 7
Tylewood SS7: Hadl'gh 3J 29
Tylney Av. SS4: R'fd 1C 22
Tyms Way SS6: Ray 7J 11
Tyndale Cl. SS5: Hull 7H 7
Tyndale Ho. SS5: Hull 7H 7
Tyrells SS5: Hock 6D 12
Tyrells, The SS17: Corr 4G 37
Tyrone Cl. CM11: Bill 7A 4
Tyrone Rd. CM11: Bill 7A 4
SS1: Sth S 6A 34
Tyrrel Dr. SS1: Sth S 5F 33
Tyrrell Ct. SS13: Pit 6G 17
Tyrrell Rd. SS7: Ben 3B 28
Tyrrells Rd. CM11: Bill 7B 4
Tythe Barn Way CM3: Sth F 2G 7

U

Ullswater Rd. SS7: Thun 5E 18
Ulster Av. SS3: Shoe 6C 34
Ulting Way SS11: Wick 3J 9
Ulverston Rd. SS4: Ashin 2J 13
Una Rd. SS13: B Gif 6K 17
Undercliff Gdns. SS9: Lgh S 5H 31
Underhill Rd. SS7: Ben 2E 28
Underwood Sq. SS9: Lgh S 3E 30
Union La. SS4: R'fd 2C 22
University of Essex
The Gateway Building 5E 32
University Sq. SS1: Sth S 5D 32
Upland Cl. CM12: Bill 3E 4
Upland Dr. CM12: Bill 3D 4
Upland Rd. CM12: Bill 3D 4
SS9: Lgh S 5J 31
Uplands Cl. SS5: Hawk 6F 13
SS7: Ben 2B 28
Uplands Pk. Ct. SS6: Ray 1A 20
Uplands Pk. Rd. SS6: Ray 7H 11
Uplands Rd. SS5: Hawk 6F 13
SS7: Ben 2B 28
Upper Av. SS13: B Gif 4J 17
Upper Lambricks SS6: Ray 7J 11
Upper Mkt. Rd. SS12: Wick 3F 9
Upper Mayne SS15: Lain 3G 15
Upper Pk. Rd. SS12: Wick 7F 9
Upton Cl. SS17: Stan H 5D 36
Upway SS6: Ray 1K 19
Upway, The SS14: Bas 5K 15
Urmond Rd. SS8: Can I 4E 38
Uttons Av. SS9: Lgh S 5F 31
Uxbridge Cl. SS11: Wick 5H 9

V

Vaagen Rd. SS8: Can I 4F 39
Vadsoe Rd. SS8: Can I 3E 38
Vale, The CM4: Stock 1H 5
SS16: Vange 2B 26
Vale Av. SS2: Sth S 3E 32
Vale Ct. CM4: Bill 1H 5
Valence Way SS16: Lan H 7E 14
Valentines SS12: Wick 5F 9
Valerie Ho. *SS9: Lgh S* *3G 31*
(off Station Rd.)
Valkyrie Rd. SS0: Wclf S 5B 32
Vallance Cl. SS2: Sth S 2J 33
Valley Rd. CM11: Bill 5F 5
Valmar Av. SS17: Stan H 6B 36
Vanderbilt Av. SS6: Ray 3G 11
Vanderwalt Av. SS8: Can I 5H 39
Van Diemens Pass SS8: Can I 5K 39
VANGE 1D 26
Vange Bells Cnr. SS17: Fob 4K 25
Vange By-Pass
SS16: Fob, Pit, Vange 3B 26
Vange Cnr. Dr. SS16: Vange 4K 25
Vange Hill Ct. SS16: Vange 2C 26
Vange Hill Dr. SS16: Vange 7B 16
Vange Pk. Rd. SS16: Vange 3K 25
Vange Riverview Cen.
SS16: Vange *1D 26*
(off High Rd.)
Vanguards, The SS3: Shoe 5F 35
(not continuous)
Vanguard Way SS3: Shoe 5F 35
Vanguard Way Ind. Est.
SS3: Shoe 5E 34
Vantage Ct. SS2: Sth S 3E 32
Vardon Dr. SS9: Lgh S 2C 30
Vaughan Av. SS2: Sth S 4H 33
Vaughan Cl. SS4: R'fd 6K 13
Vaughan Williams Rd.
SS15: Lain 4E 14
Vaulx Rd. SS8: Can I 4F 39
Venables Cl. SS8: Can I 4G 39
Venables Ct. SS8: Can I 4G 39
Venlo Rd. SS8: Can I 3F 39
Vera Rd. CM11: D'ham 1C 8
Verbena Gdns. SS15: Lain 6E 14
Verlander Dr. SS6: Ray 4F 11
Vermeer Cres. SS3: Shoe 4G 35
Vermont Cl. SS13: Bas 4G 17
Vernon Av. SS6: Ray 7F 11
Vernon Ct. SS9: Lgh S 4E 30
Vernon Rd. SS9: Lgh S 4E 30
Vernons Wlk. SS14: Bas 4D 16
Vestry Cl. SS15: Lain 5E 14
Vicarage Cl. SS8: Can I 5B 38
SS15: Lain 6E 14
Vicarage Ct. CM0: S'min 6G 41
Vicarage Hgts. SS7: Ben 4E 28
Vicarage Hill SS7: Ben 4D 28
Vicarage Mdw. CM0: S'min 6G 41
Viceroy Ct. SS0: Wclf S 6K 31
Vickers Rd. SS2: Sth S 6B 22
Victor Av. SS13: Pit 6H 17
Victor Dr. SS9: Lgh S 5H 31
Victor Gdns. SS5: Hawk 6F 13
Victoria Av. SS2: Sth S 2C 32
SS6: Ray 7F 11
SS12: Wick 3E 8
SS16: Bas 2E 24
Victoria Bus. Pk. SS2: Sth S 3E 32
Victoria Cl. SS15: Lain 5D 14
Victoria Ct. *SS0: Wclf S* *6C 32*
(off Tower Ct. M.)
SS2: Sth S 4D 32
SS11: Wick 6J 9
SS16: Lan H *7E 14*
(off Milton Grn.)
SS17: Stan H 5C 36
Victoria Cres. SS12: Wick 4D 8
SS15: Lain 4D 14
Victoria Dr. SS3: Gt W 2J 35
SS9: Lgh S 4G 31
Victoria Rd. CM3: Sth F 4H 7
SS1: Sth S 5G 33
SS6: Ray 1A 20
SS9: Lgh S 5G 31
SS15: Lain 5C 14
SS16: Vange 3B 26
SS17: Stan H 6C 36
Victoria Shop. Cen., The
SS2: Sth S 5E 32
Victor Mew Cl. SS12: Wick 6F 9
Victory Cl. SS11: Wick 6J 9
Victory La. SS4: Ashin 5K 13
Victory Path SS0: Wclf S 5K 31
Vikings Way SS8: Can I 5B 38
Viking Way SS11: Runw 1F 9
Village Dr. SS8: Can I 5C 38
Village Hall Cl. SS8: Can I 5B 38
Villa Rd. SS7: Ben 1B 28
Villiers Way SS7: Thun 7F 19
Vincent Av. SS17: Horn H 4A 36
Vincent Cl. SS3: Shoe 5E 34
SS17: Corr 4H 37
Vincent Lodge CM3: Sth F 4J 7
Vincent M. SS3: Shoe 5E 34
Vincent Rd. SS5: Hock 2H 13
Vincent Way CM12: Bill 2D 4
Vine Cl. SS14: Bas 6C 16
Vintners, The SS2: Sth S 7D 22
Viola Cl. SS15: Lain 7E 14
Virgin Active
Benfleet 7J 19
Virginia Cl. SS7: Thun 5B 18
Vista Rd. SS11: Wick 4H 9
Voorburg Rd. SS8: Can I 5H 39
Voorne Av. SS8: Can I 6H 39
Vowler Rd. SS16: Lan H 1D 24
Voysey Gdns. SS13: Bas 3F 17

W

Waalwyk Dr. SS8: Can I 4G 39
Waarden Rd. SS8: Can I 4E 38
Waarem Av. SS8: Can I 4E 38
Wadham Pk. Av. SS5: Hock 2A 12
Wakefield Av. CM12: Bill 5E 4
Wakering Av. SS3: Shoe 5G 35
Wakering Rd.
SS1: Gt W, Sth S 2A 34
SS3: Gt W 2A 34
SS3: Shoe 4G 35
Wakes Colne SS11: Wick 5J 9
Waldegrave SS16: Bas 7K 15
Waldringfield SS14: Bas 5K 15
Walk, The CM12: Bill 6E 4
SS5: Hull 7H 7
Walker Dr. SS9: Lgh S 3C 30
Walkers Sq. SS17: Stan H 6D 36
Walkey Way SS3: Shoe 5H 35
Walkways SS8: Can I 3D 38
Wallace Cl. SS5: Hull 7H 7
Wallace Dr. SS12: Wick 6G 9
Wallace St. SS3: Shoe 5F 35
Wallis Av. SS2: Sth S 3D 32
Wall Rd. SS8: Can I 5K 39

62 A-Z Southend-on-Sea

Walman Ho.—Winstree Rd.

Walman Ho. CM12: Bill 6E 4
Walnut Cl. SS15: Lain 3E 14
Walnut Ct. SS5: Hock 4E 12
Walpole Wlk. *SS6: Ray* *2C 20*
(off Bramfield Rd. E.)
Walsingham Cl. SS15: Lain 5E 14
Walsingham Rd. SS2: Sth S 2F 33
Walsingham Way CM12: Bill 2F 5
Walters Cl. SS9: Lgh S 6G 21
Waltham Ct. SS0: Wclf S 5A 32
Waltham Cres. SS2: Sth S 2F 33
Waltham Rd. SS6: Ray 1H 19
Walthams SS13: Pit 5F 17
Walthams Pl. SS13: Pit 5F 17
Walton Ct. SS15: Lain 4E 14
Walton Heath Cl.
SS17: Stan H 7B 36
Walton Rd. SS1: Sth S 7K 33
Wambrook SS3: Shoe 3D 34
Wamburg Rd. SS8: Can I 4J 39
Wansfell Gdns. SS1: Sth S 4K 33
Warburtons SS17: Stan H 4G 37
Ward Cl. SS15: Lain 7F 15
Warner Cl. CM11: Bill 6H 5
Warners Bri. Chase SS4: R'fd 6D 22
Warners Bridge Pk. 6D 22
Warners Gdns. SS2: Sth S 6C 22
Warren, The CM12: Bill 3C 4
SS17: Stan H 7E 36
Warren Chase SS7: Thun 1G 29
Warren Cl. SS6: Ray 4J 19
Warren Dr. SS11: Wick 3J 9
SS14: Bas 6C 16
Warrene Cl. SS17: Stan H 6D 36
Warren Rd. SS9: Lgh S 2C 30
Warrington Sq. CM12: Bill 4C 4
Warrior Sq. SS1: Sth S 5E 32
Warrior Sq. E. SS1: Sth S 5E 32
Warrior Sq. Nth. SS1: Sth S 5E 32
Warrior Sq. Rd. SS3: Shoe 7F 35
Warwick Cl. SS6: Ray 3B 20
SS7: Thun 5D 18
SS8: Can I 3E 38
Warwick Ct. CM0: Bur C 6C 40
Warwick Cres. SS15: Lain 3C 14
Warwick Dr. SS4: R'fd 5D 22
Warwick Gdns. SS6: Ray 3B 20
Warwick Grn. SS6: Ray 3C 20
Warwick Pde. CM3: Sth F 2H 7
Warwick Pl. SS16: Lan H 1B 24
Warwick Rd. SS1: Sth S 7K 33
SS6: Ray 3A 20
Washington Av. SS15: Lain 6C 14
Wash Rd. SS15: Bas, Lain 3F 15
Wash Rd. W. SS15: Bas, Lain 2E 14
Watchfield La. SS6: Ray 3J 19
Waterdene SS8: Can I 3C 38
Waterfalls, The SS16: Lan H 2D 24
Waterford Rd. SS3: Shoe 6D 34
Waterfront Wlk. SS14: Bas 4K 15
Waterhale SS1: Sth S 3A 34
Waterloo Rd. SS3: Shoe 5D 34
Waters Edge SS0: Wclf S 6B 32
Watersedge SS8: Can I 3J 39
Waterside SS1: Sth S 7H 33
Waterside Farm Leisure Cen. 2C 38
Waterside Mead SS8: Can I 2D 38
Waters Mead SS1: Sth S 5A 34
Waterville Dr. SS16: Vange 1E 26
Waterworks La. SS17: Fob 1J 37
Watery La. SS11: Raw, Ray 2F 11
Watkins Cl. SS13: Bas 3H 17
Watkins Way SS3: Shoe 3F 35
Watlington Rd. SS7: Ben 3B 28
Watson Cl. SS3: Shoe 5D 34
Watts La. SS4: R'fd 3D 22
Wat Tyler Country Pk. 4F 27
Waverley Cres. SS11: Runw 1E 8
Waverley Rd. SS7: Thun 6C 18
SS15: Lain 3G 15
Wavertree Rd. SS7: Ben 1B 28
Waxwell Rd. SS5: Hull 1J 11
Wayfarer Gdns. CM0: Bur C 5B 40
Wayletts SS9: Lgh S 6D 20
SS15: Lain 4C 14
Weald, The SS8: Can I 4C 38
Weare Gifford SS3: Shoe 4C 34
Weaverdale SS3: Shoe 3D 34
Weavers SS16: Vange 1D 26
Weavers Cl. CM11: Bill 5F 5
Webster Rd. SS17: Stan H 5E 36
Websters Way SS6: Ray 2K 19
Wedds Way SS3: Gt W 1H 35
Wedgwood Ct. SS4: Ashin 5K 13
Wedgwood Way SS4: Ashin 5J 13
Weelkes Cl. SS17: Stan H 4C 36
Weel Rd. SS8: Can I 6H 39
WEIR 4J 19
Weirbrook SS6: Thun 4H 19
Weir Farm Rd. SS6: Ray 4J 19
Weir Gdns. SS6: Ray 3J 19
Weir Pond Rd. SS4: R'fd 2D 22
Weir Wynd CM12: Bill 6E 4
Welbeck Cl. SS5: Hawk 7F 13
Welbeck Dr. SS16: Lan H 1C 24
Welbeck Ri. SS16: Lan H 1C 24
Welbeck Rd. SS8: Can I 6E 38
Welch Cl. SS2: Sth S 3J 33
Welcome Ct. SS17: Stan H 6C 36
Welland Rd. CM0: Bur C 4B 40
Wellingbury SS7: Ben 7C 18
Wellington Av. SS0: Wclf S 4J 31
SS5: Hull 3H 11
Wellington M. CM12: Bill 2E 4
Wellington Rd. SS5: Hock 2F 13
SS6: Ray 7K 11
Wellingtons, The CM0: S'min 6G 41
Well Mead CM12: Bill 6A 4
Wells Av. SS2: Sth S 6B 22
Wellsfield SS6: Ray 7J 11
Wells Gdns. SS14: Bas 4D 16
Wellstead Gdns. SS0: Wclf S 2K 31
Wellstye Grn. SS14: Bas 4C 16
Welton Way SS4: R'fd 3E 22
Wendene SS16: Vange 1D 26
Wendon Cl. SS4: R'fd 7J 13
Wenham Dr. SS0: Wclf S 3C 32
Wensley Rd. SS7: Thun 1H 29
Wentworth Rd. SS2: Sth S 2E 32
SS17: Stan H 7B 36
Wesley Ct. SS1: Sth S 5F 33
Wesley Gdns. CM12: Bill 2D 4
Wesley Rd. SS1: Sth S 6F 33
Wessem Rd. SS8: Can I 3F 39
West Av. SS5: Hull 7G 7
SS16: Lan H 1A 24
W. Beech Av. SS11: Wick 4F 9
W. Beech Cl. SS11: Wick 4G 9
W. Beech M. SS11: Wick 4F 9
WESTBOROUGH 4C 32
Westborough Rd. SS0: Wclf S 3K 31
Westbourne Cl. SS5: Hock 4G 13
SS7: Hadl'gh 7K 19
Westbourne Gdns. CM12: Bill 2F 5
Westbourne Gro. SS0: Wclf S 4K 31
Westbury SS4: R'fd 7J 13
Westbury Rd. SS2: Sth S 3G 33
Westcliff Av. SS0: Wclf S 6C 32
Westcliff Dr. SS9: Lgh S 4F 31
Westcliff Gdns. SS8: Can I 6J 39
WESTCLIFF-ON-SEA 6B 32
Westcliff Pde. SS0: Wclf S 6C 32
Westcliff Pk. Dr. SS0: Wclf S 4B 32
Westcliff Station (Rail) 5B 32
West Cloister CM11: Bill 5F 5
West Cres. SS8: Can I 4D 38
West Cft. CM11: Bill 5F 5
Westerings, The SS5: Hawk 6E 12
Westerland Av. SS8: Can I 4H 39
Western Approaches
SS2: Sth S 5H 21
Western Esplanade
SS0: Wclf S 6A 32
SS1: Sth S 6A 32
SS8: Can I 6F 39
Western Link Rd. SS15: Lain 4A 14
Western M. CM12: Bill 5E 4
Western Rd. CM0: Bur C 6C 40
CM12: Bill 6D 4
SS6: Ray 4H 19
SS7: Hadl'gh 6A 20
SS9: Lgh S 4C 30
Western Vw. CM12: Bill 6D 4
Westfield SS15: Lain 4C 14
Westfield Cl. SS6: Ray 6F 11
SS11: Wick 3H 9
Westfleet Trad. Est.
SS11: Wick 5H 9
Westgate SS3: Shoe 6E 34
SS14: Bas 6J 15
Westgate Pk. SS14: Bas 7J 15
West Grn. SS7: Ben 7B 18
West Hook SS16: Lan H 2B 24
West Ho. Est. CM0: S'min 5F 41
Westlake Av. SS13: B Gif 6J 17
Westleigh Av. SS9: Lgh S 3F 31
Westleigh Ct. *SS9: Lgh S* *4F 31*
(off Westleigh Av.)
West Ley CM0: Bur C 5D 40
Westley Rd. SS16: Bas 3E 24
Westman Rd. SS8: Can I 5J 39
Westmarch CM3: Sth F 4G 7
West Mayne SS15: Lain 5A 14
Westmayne Ind. Pk.
SS15: Lain 6A 14
Westmede SS16: Lan H 1E 24
Westminster Dr. SS0: Wclf S 4K 31
SS5: Hock 5C 12
Westminster Mans.
SS0: Wclf S 3K 31
Weston Chambers *SS1: Sth S* *6E 32*
(off Weston Rd.)
Weston Rd. SS1: Sth S 6E 32
West Pk. Av. CM12: Bill 4E 4
West Pk. Cres. CM12: Bill 5E 4
West Pk. Dr. CM12: Bill 5E 4
W. Point Pl. SS8: Can I 5A 38
Westray Wlk. SS12: Wick 6J 9
West Ridge CM12: Bill 7E 4
West Rd. SS0: Wclf S 4B 32
SS3: Shoe 5D 34
West Rd. Ho. SS0: Wclf S 3C 32
West St. SS2: Sth S 3C 32
SS4: R'fd 2C 22
SS9: Lgh S 5G 31
West Thorpe SS14: Bas 6A 16
West Vw. Dr. SS6: Ray 3H 19
Westwater SS7: Ben 1B 28
Westway CM3: Sth F 3G 7
SS3: Shoe 6E 34
W. Wood Cl. SS7: Thun 1J 29
Westwood Ct. SS7: Hadl'gh 1K 29
Westwood Gdns.
SS7: Hadl'gh 1K 29
Westwood Lodge
SS7: Hadl'gh 7J 19
Westwood Rd. SS8: Can I 5F 39
Wetherland SS16: Bas 7H 15
Wethersfield Cl. SS6: Ray 1G 19
Wethersfield Way SS11: Wick 6K 9
Weybourne Cl. SS2: Sth S 2F 33
Weybourne Gdns. SS2: Sth S 2F 33
Weybridge Wlk. SS3: Shoe 3E 34
Weydale SS17: Corr 2H 37
Weymarks SS15: Lain 5F 15
Wharf Cl. SS17: Stan H 6D 36
Wharf La. SS16: Pit 3D 26
Wharf Rd. SS17: Fob 3K 37
SS17: Stan H 6D 36
Wheatear Pl. CM11: Bill 6G 5
Wheatfield Way SS16: Lan H 1C 24
Wheatley Cl. SS4: R'fd 7K 13
Wheatley Rd. SS17: Corr 2H 37
Wheaton Av. SS16: Lan H 2C 24
Wheelers La. SS17: Fob 2K 37
Wheelwrights, The
SS2: Sth S 7E 22
Whernside Av. SS8: Can I 3G 39
Whinhams Way CM12: Bill 4D 4
Whist Av. SS11: Wick 2H 9
Whistler Ri. SS3: Shoe 4G 35
Whitcroft SS16: Lan H 2E 24
Whitefriars Cres. SS0: Wclf S 5A 32
Whitegate Rd. SS1: Sth S 5E 32
Whitehall La. SS17: Fob 6A 26
Whitehall Rd. SS3: Gt W 1H 35
White Hart La.
SS5: Hawk, Hock 6E 12
White Ho. Chase SS6: Ray 3A 20
White Ho. Ct. SS6: Ray 3A 20
Whitehouse Mdws.
SS9: Lgh S 6J 21
Whitehouse M. SS6: Ray 3A 20
Whitehouse Rd. CM3: Sth F 2H 7
SS9: Lgh S, Sth S 6H 21
Whitelands Cl. SS11: Wick 2G 9
White Rd. SS8: Can I 5A 38
Whiteshott SS16: Bas 1J 25
Whitesmith Dr. CM12: Bill 4C 4
White Tree Ct. CM3: Sth F 4F 7
Whiteways CM11: Bill 5J 5
SS8: Can I 6H 39
SS9: Lgh S 6H 21
Whitfields SS17: Stan H 5F 37
Whitmore Ct. SS14: Bas 4C 16
Whitmore Way SS14: Bas 5K 15
Whittingham Av. SS2: Sth S 3J 33
Whittingham Ho. SS2: Sth S 3J 33
Whybrews SS17: Stan H 5F 37
Whytewaters SS16: Vange 2D 26
Wick Beech Av. SS11: Wick 4G 9
Wick Chase SS2: Sth S 3J 33
Wick Country Pk., The 7H 9
Wick Cres. SS12: Wick 6G 9
Wick Dr. SS12: Wick 4F 9
(North Cres.)
SS12: Wick 6G 9
(Salcott Cres.)
WICKFORD 4F 9
Wickford Av. SS13: Pit 6E 16
Wickford Bus. Pk. SS11: Wick 5H 9
(not continuous)
Wickford Ct. SS13: Pit 6E 16
Wickford M. SS13: Pit 6E 16
Wickford Pl. SS13: Pit 6E 16
Wickford Rd. CM3: Sth F 2E 6
SS0: Wclf S 6C 32
Wickford Station (Rail) 3F 9
Wickford Swim & Fitness Cen. 3E 8
Wick Glen CM12: Bill 3D 4
Wickham Bus. Pk. SS14: Bas 2D 16
Wickham Pl. SS16: Bas 7A 16
Wickhay SS15: Lain 7H 15
Wick La. SS11: Wick 4G 9
(not continuous)
Wicklow Wlk. SS3: Shoe 5C 34
Wickmead Cl. SS2: Sth S 3J 33
Wick Rd. CM0: Bur C 6E 40
Widgeons SS13: Pit 6G 17
Wiggin's La. CM12: Bill, L Bur 7C 4
Wilkin Ct. SS9: Lgh S 3F 31
Wilkinson Drop SS7: Hadl'gh 3A 30
William Grn. SS5: Hull 7J 7
William Rd. SS13: B Gif 6K 17
Williamsons Way SS17: Corr 2F 37
Willingale Av. SS6: Ray 1G 19
Willingales, The SS15: Lain 6C 14
Willingale Way SS1: Sth S 3A 34
Willison Way SS7: Thun 7H 19
Willmott Rd. SS2: Sth S 6B 22
Willow Cl. CM0: Bur C 4C 40
SS5: Hock 5F 13
SS6: Ray 7H 11
SS8: Can I 5D 38
SS9: Lgh S 6H 21
Willow Ct. SS12: Wick 3E 8
Willowdale Cen. SS12: Wick 3F 9
Willow Dr. SS6: Ray 7G 11
Willowend SS8: Can I 4J 39
Willowfield SS15: Lain 4E 14
Willow Gro. CM3: Sth F 1E 6
Willow Hill SS17: Stan H 2E 36
Willow Lodge *SS7: Thun* *6F 19*
(off Hart Rd.)
Willows, The CM11: Bill 6B 4
SS1: Sth S 3A 34
SS7: Ben 1B 28
SS13: Pit 6G 17
Willow Wlk. SS5: Hock 5F 13
SS7: Hadl'gh 2K 29
Wills Hill SS17: Stan H 4D 36
Wilmott Cl. SS14: Bas 6J 15
Wilmslowe SS8: Can I 3H 39
Wilrich Av. SS8: Can I 5H 39
Wilsner SS13: Pit 5G 17
Wilson Cl. SS17: Stan H 7C 36
Wilson Ct. SS12: Wick 5E 8
Wilson Rd. SS1: Sth S 6D 32
Wimarc Cres. SS6: Ray 7F 11
Wimbish Ct. SS13: Pit 5F 17
Wimbish End SS13: Pit 6F 17
Wimbish M. SS13: Pit 5F 17
Wimborne Rd. SS2: Sth S 4F 33
Wimbourne SS15: Lain 5C 14
Wimhurst Cl. SS5: Hock 4E 12
Winbrook Cl. SS6: Ray 4A 20
Winbrook Rd. SS6: Ray 4A 20
Winchcombe Cl. SS9: Lgh S 2G 31
Winchester Cl. SS9: Lgh S 5H 21
Winchester Dr. SS6: Ray 5F 11
Winchester Gdns. SS15: Lain 3E 14
Wincoat Cl. SS7: Ben 2C 28
Wincoat Dr. SS7: Ben 2C 28
Windermere Av. SS5: Hull 1G 11
Windermere Rd. SS1: Sth S 5G 33
SS7: Thun 5E 18
Windmill Hgts. CM12: Bill 7F 5
Windmill Steps *SS1: Sth S* *6G 33*
(off Kursaal Way)
Windsor Av. SS17: Corr 2G 37
Windsor Cl. SS8: Can I 5F 39
SS9: Lgh S 2G 31
Windsor Gdns. SS5: Hawk 7H 13
SS7: Thun 1J 29
SS11: Runw 2F 9
Windsor M. SS6: Ray 3J 19
Windsor Rd. SS0: Wclf S 4C 32
SS13: B Gif 4J 17
Windsor Way SS6: Ray 3A 20
Windward Way CM3: Sth F 4K 7
Winfields SS13: Pit 5G 17
Winifred Rd. SS13: Pit 6F 17
Winnowers Ct. SS4: R'fd 2D 22
Winsford Gdns. SS0: Wclf S 1J 31
Winstanley Way SS14: Bas 4J 15
Winstree SS13: Bas 4F 17
Winstree Rd. CM0: Bur C 5C 40

A-Z Southend-on-Sea 63

SAFETY CAMERA INFORMATION

PocketGPSWorld.com's CamerAlert is a self-contained speed and red light camera warning system for
SatNavs and Android or Apple iOS smartphones/tablets. Visit www.cameralert.com to download.

Safety camera locations are publicised by the Safer Roads Partnership which operates them in order to encourage drivers to comply
with speed limits at these sites. It is the driver's absolute responsibility to be aware of and to adhere to speed limits at all times.

By showing this safety camera information it is the intention of Geographers' A-Z Map Company Ltd. to encourage
safe driving and greater awareness of speed limits and vehicle speed. Data accurate at time of printing.